The Art of a Loving Relationship

An Enlightening Book on Relationships for Women and Men to Master Love and Mindful Connections

S. Morteza Lajevardi

Peace and Love Institute
Montreal, Canada

Published by Peace and Love Institute
www.PeaceAndLoveInstitute.com
First edition, 2024

Paperback ISBN: 978-1-7382419-8-9
E-book ISBN: 978-1-7382419-6-5
Hardcover ISBN: 978-1-7382419-7-2

Peace and Love Institute
Montreal, Canada

Oh amazing love!
Let me sing of your wonders.
With these words,
Let me open a door into light.

—Rumi

Contents

Chapter 1

What Love Is

On a beautiful day at the beginning of spring, I entered the metro station in Montreal, Canada. The metro station was not crowded. While waiting for the train to arrive, I suddenly noticed an older couple leaning on the wall; the man's arm hung lovingly over his beloved's shoulder. The posture and feeling were so beautiful that I could sense the energy of love flowing between them from the distance.

At first, I hesitated to talk with them, but I overcame my hesitation and approached them. I said, "Hi, may I ask you a question? I am an author and am preparing to write about love and relationships." The old man looked at me for a few seconds and said, "Okay, what do you want to know?" I asked, "Would you please tell me how long you have been together and the secret of your loving relationship?" He said they have been together for 54 years and continued, "The secret of our loving relationship is the decision to love every day." Immediately, his wife said, in French, "Patience." I wanted to talk more, but the train arrived, and we entered the connected wagons. Our conversation ended, but I got the gist. I felt good and was content to learn a beautiful lesson from a loving couple who provided a living exemplar of true love in the modern age.

What Is Love?

Years ago, I heard what love is from Abbas Kiarostami, a prominent Iranian film producer and award-winning director of the Cannes Film Festival. He told a simple yet eye-opening story. He said someone asked a child, "What is love?" The child answered, "Liking very much."

Love is simple, meaning liking someone or something very much, but it is also complex. As each human's inner world is different, each person's feelings and meaning of love are different.

From a spiritual perspective, love is to emigrate from *self*, expand from within, and merge with another person or anything in the universe to become *one*. The concept of *oneness* is at the core of true love. Duality causes separation, and *oneness* creates unity. The need to love and to be loved has been ingrained in the human emotional mind. It is the foundation of existence. We can observe the unconditional love of a mother for her baby. A mother loves her baby without any effort to acquire this love. Love has already been embedded in her being, and when her baby is born, the love manifests itself in its purest form without judgment and expectations. Love is an opportunity to say *no* to the ego and let the higher human traits manifest.

In another interesting story, a lover knocked on the door of his beloved's home. The beloved asked, "Who are you?" "It's me, your lover," he replied. The beloved responded, "Your love isn't mature yet; don't come in." The lover wondered, and after years of the inner journey, he came back and knocked on the door of his beloved's home. His beloved said, "Who are you?" This time, matured in love and understanding, the lover said, "It's you." The beloved promptly said, "You got it! Come in!"[1]

When you enter the love world, you see your beloved as an opportunity to give because pleasure is greater in giving than receiving. This point is one of the key factors of true love: giving without expectations because pleasure is in giving. The pleasure is to let the superficial needs of ego disappear and let the beauty of a higher level of humanity emerge and lighten life. As Hafiz beautifully describes the true love in his poem:

Even after all this time,
The Sun never says to the Earth,

---

[1] Rumi poetry collection

"You owe me."
Look what happens,
With a love like that,
It lights the whole sky.

In true love, when I am not an *I* anymore, you are not a *you* anymore, and we become *we*, the relationship is in its affinity, fondness, and joy.

What Are the Characteristics of True Love?

Love begins without *I*, and a relationship is an opportunity to give and grow. Honest caring is absolutely an essential aspect of true love. The well-being of your beloved should be a high priority in your life. The concern won't be anymore, "What do I want?" but "What does my beloved want?"

When the happiness of your beloved is your happiness,
When just gazing at your beloved is all you want,
When you attentively listen to your beloved,
When you genuinely compliment and admire your beloved,
When you focus on giving without any expectations,
When you accept everything about your beloved, including good things and flaws,
When you enjoy when your beloved enjoys,
When you compromise wholeheartedly,
When your beloved's smile is a great gift for you,
When you decide at every moment to love,
When you decide at every moment to commit,

> When you don't stop knowing your beloved,
> When you trust your beloved,
> When you respect your beloved's decisions,
> When you are responsive to your beloved's emotional needs, you are truly in love.

You can add more to this list to define what love means to you. It sounds intimidating, right? However, loving is the most beautiful feeling one can experience; it is one of the highest levels of humanity; and thus, it isn't easy. But the pleasure of love is so beautiful and joyful that even its pain has some flavor of ecstasy. As Hafiz said in his poem:

> O Tapster! Bring the cup and give me the wine,
> Love appeared to be easy at first glimpse,
> But difficulties came after.

Every human has the capacity to love; however, for some people, it is easier to love, while for others, it requires more inner work to let the light within pass through the thick curtains of the *false self* or the ego. You can decide to learn to love and develop the characteristics of a true lover. Like any other personal and interpersonal skill, the first step is insight: self-awareness and increasing knowledge about what true love is and what it isn't. The art of loving is learnable, and one can develop the highest level of humanity and grow in altruism and spiritual realms. True love erupts from within; it is deep, unconditional, and perpetual; it is connected to the Infinite Love within; it is life, a feeling that transcends time and space.

False love, on the other hand, is conditional and egoistic. It brings superficial pleasure but not the authentic joy of true love. False love is learned from others and is a human-made definition of love; true love has been and will be forever.

In true love, a lover's mindset actively looks for the ways that he can give, not actively looking for what he can get.[2] A lover's giving bears no expectations because expectations in a relationship are a trade, not love. A lover has great capacity within and is full of self-love, self-respect, and self-acceptance, so she wants to share love, respect, and acceptance with another human.

But what about other people's destructive behavior toward unconditional love? First, everybody is responsible for their own behavior and actions. If you freely choose to love, true love has essential qualities. You are free to choose whom you want to share your love with, but it should be unconditional when you give your love. Giving, caring, compassion, kindness, respect, and being responsive to the emotional well-being of your beloved are essential in a loving relationship.

What causes the desire to love and to be loved? Separateness is not what a human naturally wants. The desire for *oneness* and *unity* urges one to look for love and to

---

[2] Hereinafter, I use pronouns *She* and *He* interchangeably to refer to third person.

be loved. It is natural for human beings to seek connections; it is not normal for them to be isolated and detached.

When we love someone, we should have discipline; there should be some regulations to protect our love. The decision to love in every moment sounds too good to be true, but it is possible through faithful commitment. Many couples around the world are experiencing true love, and statistics show this is true. So, anyone can experience true love through discipline and a commitment to follow and respect true love's requirements. Having faith in oneself, your relationship, and your partner is crucial, as the certainty and sureness in your heart make it possible for you to step on the path of true love, leading to emotional and personal growth.

True love demands your presence and mental energy. Faith is simply a mental state in which one's heart is sure and certain. Fulfilling anything worthwhile in life requires faith in oneself and one's ability to act and achieve it. Experiencing true love requires having faith in true love. You have to believe that true love exists and claim it. You have to pay attention to your beloved and be responsive to her well-being. You should learn how to live in the present moment and enjoy each other's companionship. Like learning any kind of art, learning the art of loving requires practicing to acquire loving characteristics such as being patient, attentive, responsive, responsible, kind, compassionate, and compromising. To learn the art of love, one has to be focused, determined, persistent, and patient; like learning other kinds of art, no one will become a master in love overnight. So, being patient on your path toward the happy land of love is necessary. You should pay attention and focus on learning the art of loving. Some people, though not many, are naturally more loving; however, it doesn't mean others can't develop a loving attitude in their hearts.

Patience is another crucial element in a loving relationship. Patience is different from tolerance; rather, patience accompanies peacefulness and certainty that things will eventually be all right, while tolerance follows emotional struggles and pain. In true love, even when things appear wrong, one should be patient and trust that everything will be fine. It doesn't mean to ignore facts but to have a positive perspective in difficult moments to help you stay at peace. When we are patient, we are responsive toward misbehavior and flaws, not reactive. Being reactive means responding to undesired situations quickly and spontaneously without much involvement of our conscious mind. For example, when your partner blames you, the easiest way is to become defensive and fight back. But when you are patient, you pause your reaction, reevaluate the situation, and find the best way to deal with it. The solution to extinguish a fire is not to add more fire. Being defensive when your partner blames you does not correspond with true love characteristics.

Why Humans Yearn for Quality Relationships

On a biological level, humans are programmed to connect and be together. In the evolution process, humans understood that when they were together, they were safer and had a much higher chance of survival. The need to connect to other humans is deep inside, programmed in the DNA of every human being. Even those who deliberately choose to live alone yearn for a relationship deep inside themselves but believe they can't have what they want in a relationship.

A relationship is a path to grow emotionally and spiritually. One of the main reasons for the attraction of two humans to each other is to produce offspring. Life wants to continue, and it has provided a system to bring two humans together and build a relationship to guarantee human existence on Earth. A relationship is also a profound way to grow in humanity and heal childhood wounds. It helps humans think and care beyond *self*. First, you learn to care about the person you are in a relationship with. Then, if you have kids together, you learn to care about your kids as well. So, you are growing from within, contributing from your heart to others. Some people grow even more and care about other people and the human community. So, the bigger we become from the inside, the more space we have in our heart for other humans and everything else life offers. And when our love spectrum covers more humans and things, we have grown in spirituality. Love has a purpose: a connection to everyone and everything in life and a feeling of *oneness* and *unity*. Imagine a world where everyone cared for one another; that would be the utopia. Love begins within oneself through self-love and expands from within. Loving another human makes more room in your heart to become a better human. The more you make room in your heart, the more loving you become.

Deep Inside a Human Being Is Pure Love

Think about a newborn baby; she is pure life and loves without judgment, comparison, prejudice, worry, sadness, or hatred. She is fresh and gives life into the environment. She is highly suggestible, and information from the environment enters her soul and forms the structure of her brain so that she can adapt to the environment in which she is growing up. This information enters the newborn subconscious mind and begins covering her core essence, which is pure life and love. She couldn't choose what information to accept and what information to reject. All constructive and destructive information entered her being and created neural pathways and circuits in her brain. By the age of two, her core personality has formed. She is learning the family and society norms and standards, and the environmental information becomes the foundation for her future comparison and judgment. The information builds her belief system through which she makes a self-image of herself and perceives others, events, and the environment. Her belief system has been formed based on environmental information, and she interprets the data she receives from the environment. If she doesn't receive enough love and care from her parents or primary caregivers, she forms a self-image of herself and perceives herself as an *unlovable* and *unworthy* being. Her attempts to connect with her parents begin with eye contact and touch. She sends messages through crying when she needs something. If her parents are responsive to her emotional and physical needs, she would perceive the world as a safe place to be, and if she doesn't receive adequate care and attention when she needs them, she perceives the world as unsafe and unreliable. If she grew up in a divorced family with a single parent, the environment may convey the message that divorce is an inevitable and a normal life experience. As the environmental information has built her belief system through which she sees the world, her experiences will continue to reinforce her beliefs because the mind works all the time to prove its reliability and confirm what it has accepted as truth.

If the child has developed a poor self-image of unworthiness and unlovability, people will treat her as unworthy and unlovable to confirm her unworthy and unlovable self-image. Her belief system makes her expectations about life and relationships and detaches her from her core being. She becomes closer to her core being when she stops comparing herself with others and does not judge or belittle herself. When she starts to be in the present moment, becomes conscious of the flow of life, and controls her mind not to be distracted by thoughts, the future, and the past, she becomes closer to her true essence. She becomes closer to her core being when she begins to appreciate her being. She becomes closer to her real self when she does not prejudice or predict the future based on her past experiences and stays hopeful and open to coming fantastic possibilities. When she begins to connect with her true being and emanates love to her environment and surrounding people, she finds out that she is connected with the Infinite Love within, the same way she first came to this life as a newborn baby. When she stops overthinking and starts living in the present moment to experience the world with all her five senses, she connects to the natural current of existence and her core being, which is pure love.

Acceptance of Your Partner Comes from True Love

The passionate love in a long-term relationship changes eventually to compassionate love. In compassionate love, what is important is to accept your beloved with all his good traits and flaws. You are not going to judge or nag your partner for what he has done wrong or his flaws; instead, you try to understand your partner and accept him for who he is. Your partner may or may not be aware of his flaws and might resist any change or advice, but you should understand that we are all humans, and everyone has some bad habits and flaws, even if he is not aware of them. Every time a woman nags and criticizes her man, she unknowingly damages her man's self-confidence. And whenever a man criticizes his woman, he unconsciously hurts his woman's self-esteem. Nagging and criticism in relationships are destructive habits.

Often, we cannot change others with nagging and criticism but with true love and acceptance. By your true love, the treasure of love in your partner's heart, which might have been buried under childhood and adulthood wounds, could emerge. Your partner doesn't need your nagging or criticism; he needs your understanding and acceptance. Focus on what your man is doing right and appreciate him. Excessive, unjustified advice indirectly conveys the message of incompetency and flaws to your man, conveying the message that he is not accepted the way he is and negatively impacting his testosterone level and emotional well-being. On the other hand, men should avoid any criticism of their woman and compliment her at every opportunity.

What Are the Characteristics of Disguised Love?

Clinging, controlling, a sense of ownership, and unreasonable expectations are characteristics of disguised love. The disguised love is learned; what we have heard and seen about love in the environment in which we live makes an unrealistic definition of love that is far from true love. In many love songs, the lyrics imply that a lover loves his beloved to such an extent that he cannot live without her. That means if you love someone, your existence depends on your beloved.

If you control your partner, from your perspective, you may want to express how much you love him, while controlling pushes him further from you. No one wants to be controlled; freedom is a fundamental human need. A sense of ownership goes hand in hand with controlling someone. Usually, we want to control someone when we feel we have some superior rights to do so, a sense of ownership. Respecting the freedom of your beloved results from your true love. But freedom doesn't mean violating one of the vital prerequisites of a loving relationship: commitment. Freedom means giving space to your beloved and letting him do what he wants to spend time on.

Unreasonable expectations are also a pitfall for true love; they occur when we calculate what we give and receive in a relationship. As I mentioned, in a true love relationship, we give without expectations because of love. We have already received the reward for our giving because of the pleasure of love.

A Happy Relationship

When our inner world's needs and desires are met by what we expect in our outside world, we feel a sense of exhilaration. In a relationship, when your partner fulfills your physical and emotional needs and desires for proximity, you feel a sense of vivacity. When you do pleasurable activities with your partner and feel and understand your partner, you are in harmony with the flow of life and feel no resistance. You feel good and happy. Your inner world's desire for thriving and expanding is getting what it longs for. When we are happy, we want to expand; that's why some people begin to dance, move quickly, or scream with hilarity when they experience happiness. Your desire to be in a happy relationship is embedded in your need to grow and experience the world to the fullest. With all this, you should know that true happiness begins inside you. A happy person starts a relationship to be happier and experience higher alacrity. Some experts say, "Take full responsibility for your happiness and don't rely on anyone, even your partner, to make you happy." That statement might work for some people, but it is best to have a middle way. When we are in a relationship, we are responsible for our own happiness as well as our partner's well-being because, in a loving relationship, there is no *I* and *you*; instead, there is *we*. Focusing too much on our own happiness may cause distance and accentuate *I*, not *we*.

Unrealistic expectations in a relationship can hinder relationship satisfaction and the sense of happiness. When you watch a two-hour romance movie, they condense many romantic, passionate scenes to make the movie exciting and captivating, whereas real life is not a two-hour movie. Your mind uses the romance movie as a reference and compares your daily life with your partner with that in the movie, which may result in dissatisfaction in your relationship. Everything you watch or hear becomes a memory that remains in your subconscious mind forever, even though you remember nothing of what you watched or heard. The subconscious mind uses all implicit and explicit memories to create your feelings in your current relationship.

Your expectations about your relationship are formed based on all the data you have received during your life about how a happy relationship should be. The way you developed a connection with your parents or primary caregivers and the quality of your parents' relationship with each other significantly impact your perception of your relationship with your partner and your expectations. Reexamining your expectations in a relationship and changing your perception of them can tremendously change the quality of your relationship and bring you a more satisfactory connection with your partner.

Falling in Love Versus Evolving in Love

Everything feels magical when someone falls in love. Euphoria dominates every aspect of life. You recognize your beloved, sometimes in less than 30 seconds, because your subconscious mind matches your beloved's subconscious mind, and, unlike the conscious mind, the subconscious mind is extremely fast. You feel you have known each other for many years, even though you have just met each other. You feel close to the other person, and your conscious mind doesn't know why because you have recognized each other at the subconscious and emotional level. You and your beloved have connected on an emotional level without much effort from the conscious mind. After that, the attachment system in your subconscious mind is activated, and you feel you need to be with your beloved. All the hormones, including dopamine and oxytocin, are released inside the body to facilitate the connection at both emotional and physical levels. While this seems beautiful, a lasting, loving relationship requires a deeper understanding of love. For some people, this era of excitement turns into a long-term relationship in which they feel content and safe. In other words, they mature and evolve in love. They have not fallen in love anymore, in which there is emotional fluctuation and oscillation, *but they deeply accept and appreciate one another.* They accept everything about their partner, all their good traits and flaws. They trust each other, feel safe in their relationship, and sense a state of peaceful happiness. And that is for sure a great fortune in anyone's life.

When two people fall in love, at the subconscious level, they are matched with all their good traits and flaws. However, the mind often filters the flaws at the beginning of a passionate relationship by ignoring and discounting the flaws of the new beloved. Later, in many relationships that begin with passion, the mind does the opposite to ruin the relationship. When the hormones return to their normal levels, the mind ignores or discounts the positive traits in the partner and exaggerates the flaws. Usually, this is a mind trap and should be avoided. A relationship is an opportunity to mature and evolve in love. A weak person avoids challenges, and a strong person overcomes challenges. In any relationship, there are ups and downs, and when a challenge is faced, one should perceive it as an opportunity to understand their partner and look for a solution. Sometimes, the mind can't see any solution to an issue in a relationship, which is usually because of the limited information available to the mind, not because of reality. Indeed, if you believe there is a solution to any problem, there will always be a way out of the problem.

Hormones in Compassionate Love and Romantic Love

Unlike compassionate love, which can be for more than one person, romantic love is usually for one special person. Love is a convoluted process that engages every aspect of a human being, from psyche to body. Compassionate love is usually for close family members or others who are significant in our life; it is a calm, tender feeling and feels secure.

On the other hand, romantic love is usually tense; it might induce anxiousness and cause a desperate feeling of the need to be with someone perceived as special. Studies show that compassionate love and romantic love cause the body to produce different kinds of hormones. In compassionate love, the body produces oxytocin, which makes a human feel calm, content, and secure, and vasopressin, which makes a human feel connected to build social bonds.

In romantic love, the body produces four hormones:

- Dopamine
- Noradrenaline
- Cortisol
- Serotonin

Dopamine gives the feeling of pleasure, satisfaction, and motivation. Noradrenaline is both a neurotransmitter and a hormone and plays a vital role in a human fight-or-flight response to stimuli. Cortisol is associated with stress and keeps one highly alert. Serotonin causes sexual desire and affects the mood regarding romantic relationships with hopes and fears. Often, in long-term relationships, romantic love turns to compassionate love if two people begin a close relationship and live together, as it is not natural for the body to be constantly under stress-producing cortisol hormone or noradrenaline hormone that prepares the body for a fight-or-flight reaction.

The quality of love with your partner will incline over time toward compassionate love. But you can work it out to keep the passionate love in your relationship. When you develop compassionate love and flavor it with passionate love, you grow in love, and life becomes more beautiful. There are certain strategies you can apply to maintain some degree of passion in your relationship, such as building a habit of weekly dates.

Beauty Is Relative

Beauty, especially human beauty, is relative. Someone might look beautiful to one person and be perceived as average for another person. Most people may agree that someone is very beautiful, but some might still disagree. No matter how you look, you have beauty in your personality and appearance, and you should look for those beauties, acknowledge their existence, and appreciate them. If you don't see those beauties in you and don't find yourself lovely, how can you expect others to see those beauties in you and love you?

When a woman believes she is beautiful and lovely, she engages more in behavior that helps her be beautiful and attractive. She takes care of her body and skin, eats healthy food, drinks enough water, meditates, avoids stress as much as possible, and exercises to stay fit and healthy. She finds herself beautiful and does what she can to maintain her beauty. On the other hand, when a woman has a poor self-image and perceives herself as unattractive, she engages in behavior that doesn't contribute to her beauty and sometimes may be harmful. She might eat fast food often, she might not meditate nor take care of her skin and beauty, and she doesn't wear a beautiful outfit. She might have excuses for not having time or money to care for herself. But there is always a way to eat healthily, take care of skin, and participate in activities that promote one's beauty and well-being that are free or affordable. For example, if she doesn't have money to go to the gym, she can do the best exercise known to humans: walking.

If you think you are unattractive, you should rethink, especially if it is something you have been told and believed as truth, and you are now acting according to your belief. No matter how you look, there are beauties in you, inward and outward. You should begin to behave in a way that a beautiful woman conducts. You should begin to take care of your body and skin, eat well, drink enough water, dress well, meditate, avoid stress as much as possible, and exercise. Start to view yourself as a beautiful being and appreciate your loveliness.

The Relationship Quality Index

The relationship quality index is simple. There are three major characteristics in a relationship that show how healthy a relationship is: love, kindness, and peacefulness. People often begin a relationship to feel better and experience a higher level of happiness. If you want to know the quality of your relationship, you should measure how much more love, kindness, and peacefulness you have compared to before your relationship began. A partner should contribute to one's peacefulness. A partner should be kind and compassionate. A partner should love by demonstrating trust, safety, happiness, openness, and *oneness*. No one says, "I want to begin a relationship to have less peace," or "I want to start a relationship to be angry and hateful." So, be very clear about what you want in a relationship. You can add whatever you feel you want, but the relationship quality index should be your guide for what has to be at the core of your relationship: more love, more kindness, and more peacefulness. If you are in a relationship, you can give a number from 1 to 10 (1 represents the least and 10 represents the most) to each quality index characteristic before and after your relationship and compare those numbers to see where you are in the relationship.

If you find out that you have less peace in your relationship than before, the solution isn't usually to change your partner; the solution is to find out how you both can have more peace and take continuous action to bring more peace to your relationship.

Though a relationship, like life, is a journey, it should move toward the Infinite Love, Infinite Kindness, and Infinite Peacefulness. A quality relationship should evolve in love, compassion, and attachment. Some studies show that the main thing couples want from their partner in a relationship is kindness and compassion before having good sex and helping with chores. In a loving relationship, kindness is the language of communication. Being always kind may not be easy for many, but when you know how important kindness and compassion are in a thriving relationship, you begin to work on yourself to treat your loved one with more kindness. The study of emotions shows that the primary mode of emotional communication is nonverbal. Your partner's facial expression, eyes, posture and gesture, body movements, and tone of voice communicate to you how your partner feels. An emotionally intelligent person pays careful attention to nonverbal and verbal messages from her beloved and responds to her partner's emotional needs with understanding and kindness.

Set a High Standard for Your Relationship

Setting a high standard for your relationship helps you stay on track to thrive in your connection with your partner and measure your relationship's quality. Your standard determines what qualities must be respected, included, or excluded in different areas of your relationship. What is your standard for communication? What is your standard for intimacy? What is your standard for friendship with others outside your relationship? What is your standard for loving? When you set a high standard, you should do whatever you can to respect your standard. When you plan and implement your standard in your relationship, you improve your self-image, implicitly conveying to your subconscious mind that your relationship is important to you and is a priority in your life. It also conveys the message that you are worthy of love and competent to have a loving relationship. For example, you can write down in detail how the quality of your communication with your partner should be and share it with your partner.

You want to set a high standard for your relationship so that you stay focused on what you expect from your relationship to move forward. For instance, if you expect only respectful communication from your partner, you should communicate respectfully with your partner and remind him gently that you only expect respect in return. For a loving relationship, your standard might include all the ways that you express your love and feel loved.

You can think about how you can express your love in a way that demonstrates caring, passion, and enjoyment. You can write how you feel loved and share your standard with your partner. It is okay if the quality of your current relationship doesn't correspond well with your high standard. Your relationship standard is like your guideline, helping you stay on track in improving your relationship and making your connection with your partner as good as possible. The higher your standard for a quality relationship with your partner is, the better you should work and thrive to improve your relationship. The best scenario is that you and your partner set a high standard for your relationship and work together to meet your standard. However, for whatever reason, your partner may not cooperate to set high standards for your relationship; in this case, you can set your standards and make a plan to meet your standards. Nevertheless, for some relationship criteria, you and your partner should work together to meet your standards, such as setting a standard for intimacy and connection. You can make a routine to date once a week for three hours in a pleasant environment without distraction. In a long-term relationship, setting a standard for closeness and intimacy would protect you from emotional distance and taking each other for granted. Life can get busy with work, projects, kids, personal health care, etc. Setting a high standard helps you also measure your relationship quality index—how your relationship is with respect to love, kindness, and peacefulness, and where you want it to be.

Write down below the key points you learned in Chapter 1.

Chapter 2

Beliefs, Perceptions, and Love Experience

How the Subconscious Mind Shapes Relationships

The pain-pleasure principle was developed by the prominent Austrian psychologist Sigmund Freud, and it suggests that humans consciously and unconsciously make choices to reduce or prevent pain and to increase or create pleasure. The mind, especially at the subconscious level, continuously makes choices to answer biological and psychological wants and wishes including your love relationship. The mind constantly evaluates and compares the gains and pains of being single and of being in a loving relationship and chooses a condition with the most gains and the least pains.

James is single but yearns to find his soulmate and have a quality relationship. He makes a two-column table and writes down the gains and pains of being single. He gives a score from 1 to 10 to represent the degree of importance of each gain and pain. Then, he sums each column's weights to see which one is the unconscious selection: being in a relationship or being single.

Gains of Being Single	Pains of Being Single
• Freedom: 9 • Lower expenses: 5 • Avoiding relationship conflicts: 7 • I don't need to change or compromise: 6 • I can focus on my studies and projects: 4 • Sleep more: 2 • Traveling solo: 2	• I feel lonely: 8 • I need to express my love and feel loved: 7 • I don't have emotional support: 5

As you see, the sum of the gains column is 36, while the sum of the pains column is 20. Before making the table and reflecting on its insight, he didn't think about how important freedom was for him. The pain-gain table reflects James' belief system. All his previous relationships, others' relationships, and the information he has received from his environment, including the media, have shaped how he perceives being in a quality relationship. *He unconsciously perceives being single as more enjoyable than painful,* so his mind does its best to keep him single.

James has learned about the pain-pleasure principle and decides to make a table to modify the pains' and gains' statuses in his mind. After some inner work, James has convinced himself that by being in a relationship, he won't lose all of his freedom, so he has reduced the weight of losing freedom in a relationship from 9 to 5. He has learned that any relationship will have conflicts, but conflicts are an opportunity to grow emotionally and personally by solving problems in the relationship. So, he now gives 0 to the pain of experiencing relationship conflicts. Studying how to develop a loving relationship, he also now knows that changes and compromises not only aren't a bad thing but also benefit his brain to regenerate new brain cells and stay younger. James's pain-gain table of being in a relationship is shown below.

Gains of Being in a Relationship	**Pains of Being in a Relationship**
• Love someone and to be loved: 9 • Personal growth: 4 • An opportunity for self-discovery: 4 • Good for health: 5	• Losing some degree of freedom: 5 • Higher expenses: 5 • Experiencing relationship conflicts: 0

• Emotional support: 4 • Companionship: 8 • Traveling together: 4 • Changes and compromises advantages: 4	• I can't focus on my studies and projects: 4 • Sleep less: 2 • Not traveling solo: 2

Now, the sum of the gains column of being in a relationship is 42, and the sum of the pains column of being in a relationship is 18. Now the subconscious mind has enough good reasons to look for a quality relationship, not rejecting any potential relationship for futile reasons.

To change and modify the pain-gain status in his mind so that his subconscious mind works toward having a loving relationship, James should read and contemplate the above table content a couple of times every day for at least 40 days to convince himself that by having a quality relationship he is going to gain a lot. The pain-pleasure principle can work wonderfully for you as well. You can make a pain-gain table like James's and modify your pain-gain status in your mind so your subconscious mind begins to work for you.

People with an avoidant attachment style can modify and change the pain-gain status in their mind and make the gain side heavier so their mind has enough reason to commit to and stay in a relationship (I will discuss people with an avoidant attachment style in Chapter 3).

Falling in Love Is an Unconscious Selection

When we fall in love, it feels like everything is automatically happening at the emotional level. Some programs run deep inside the human psyche that matches other human psyches. But why does the emotion of falling in love not last and instead sometimes turns into hate and break ups? Because humans fall in love through an unconscious selection and then ruin it through unconscious behaviors that are automatically guided by the subconscious mind. These behaviors reflect the inner world and usually have been formed in childhood to set boundaries in relationships with others. Still, the mind's programming works spontaneously in connection with others in adulthood. When I talk about behavior, I mean both mental and physical behaviors. Sometimes, our mental behavior isn't expressed in the outside world. However, any mental behavior is an inner-world activity, which is very important because it influences our emotions. The point is that a love relationship often begins through an unconscious selection and is unknowingly ruined through destructive behavior running in the subconscious mind. Self-awareness regarding our behavior in our relationship is a precious asset for observing our attitudes and modifying the destructive ones. When we become aware of our subconscious mind behaviors' impact on our relationship, we can consciously choose to correct those behaviors.

How a Destructive Belief about Relationships Forms

To explain the process of acquiring a destructive belief, I will tell you a story. Amanda grew up in a challenging family where her father had affairs with other women for years. Despite her father's affairs, Amanda's mother did not leave the relationship, though she was emotionally exhausted. Later, Amanda loved to watch a TV series in which the main character cheated on his wife. Amanda developed the belief that men are not biologically made for a committed relationship, and they cheat as soon as they have the opportunity to have an affair.

Amanda's mind becomes occupied with the concept of men cheating on their partner, and she activates the Reticular Activating System[3] of her mind to look for more evidence to confirm the concept that *men cheat on their partner*. She finds out that her friend's husband also has had an affair. She is now convinced that men cheat on their partner based on *her limited evidence*. What you believe, you experience. The truth is that many men are loyal and committed to their relationship; however, Amanda's Reticular Activating System overlooks the evidence which argues that there are many committed men in relationships, and it filters relationships in which men cheat on their

---

[3] The Reticular Activating System (RAS) is a network of neurons in the brainstem responsible for consciousness, focus, and motivation. RAS is also the gatekeeper of information.

partner. When a belief is ingrained in the subconscious mind, it is deeply accepted as truth and creates personal reality. Amanda will begin a relationship with a man who won't be committed and will have an affair to confirm that Amanda's belief about men is true. Beliefs are not formed overnight; they have a long history backed by life experiences confirming their truth. What you say doesn't matter much, but how you feel and what you have accepted as truth significantly affect your life. Sometimes, you may hear beautiful words and consciously like them and say them. This kind of acceptance is at the superficial level of the mind and is not part of your belief system yet. If you keep those beautiful words in your mind for a long time, contemplate them daily, and find evidence to prove their trueness to convince yourself deeply that those words are acceptable and real, you gradually ingrain those words in your subconscious mind and make them your new belief.

Amanda can change her belief about men's commitment level. She should stop watching and listening to any movies, series, or songs that show and talk about cheating and affairs. She should understand that her destructive belief is based on her limited evidence and that not all women are experiencing disloyalty in their relationships. She should find relationship role models who confirm that many men are loyal and committed to their relationship. She should write down reasons why men can be as devoted as women to their relationship and convince herself there are many faithful men. It might take Amanda a few months to gradually change her perception of men. However, she should remember that she needs to work on this constructive belief for the rest of her life, not let the destructive one reappear in the subconscious mind.

There is a myth that men are not biologically made for a committed relationship, and they cheat when they have the opportunity to have an affair. This destructive belief can affect one's life if one believes it.

Some Constructive Beliefs about Love

Beliefs are not formed overnight and evolve throughout life once they become fixed and rigid. Children growing up in a loving environment constantly learn about love. Their parents or primary caregivers are the evidence for their belief system that love exists. If the love energy that children receive is strong, negative information from the environment about relationships won't have a significant destructive effect on them.

The first prerequisite for a loving connection is to trust someone else and become reasonably vulnerable. A constructive belief regarding connection with others is to believe there are many good humans in the world. This might seem contradictory to the information we receive from the media, which usually broadcasts negativity. In the safety of isolation, one might be protected, but the big rewards are outside of the comfort zone.

Here are some constructive beliefs about love:

Love is the most beautiful feeling.
Love is real.
Love is to give without expectations.
Love erupts from within and is infinite.
I deserve to love and be loved.
I deserve a loving relationship.
There are many great men (women) to date, and I begin a wonderful, committed relationship with one of them.

How Destructive Beliefs about Love Hinder True Love

A belief system in humans is like software in a computer. Humans experience exactly what they have been programmed to be. Most human beliefs are hidden in the subconscious mind, where the conscious mind is unaware of them. In cognitive behavioral theory, belief systems have been extensively studied, and there are ways to change a belief system. In any area of life, you are experiencing exactly what you believe to be true. Any opinion you have about anything, including relationships, originated from your belief system.

What do you think about relationships?
What do you think about a long-term relationship?
What does love mean to you?
What qualities are important for you in a relationship?
What does an ideal relationship look like for you?
What are your red flags and deal breakers in a relationship?

What do you expect from your partner?
What can you contribute to a relationship?

Many other similar questions reveal layers of your belief system about relationships. But how are beliefs formed? Beliefs are simply repeated information. This repetitive information comes partially through genetic codes but mainly through the environment. The information started to enter your subconscious mind even when you were in your mother's womb. And when you were born, you began to absorb all the data from your environment through your five senses. This information created the core beliefs about who you are. The core beliefs are categorized into three main categories: lovability, worthiness, and competency. The opposites of these categories are unlovability, unworthiness, and incompetency.

Regarding relationships, every thought or behavior you engage in originates from your core beliefs about how lovable, worthy, and competent you perceive yourself, others, and your environment. In every moment, you are confirming your core beliefs through your thoughts and behavior and projecting your inner belief system onto the outside world.

If you grew up in a family where you were treated with love and respect, you developed core beliefs that you are lovable and worthy, and you will *expect* only love and respect and *reject* disrespect and indifference. Your mental filter automatically accepts what confirms your core beliefs, and it rejects any behavior that opposes your core beliefs; the problem is that our environment is polluted with negative information that builds up destructive core beliefs.

Everything you hear, watch, see, listen, touch, and smell sinks directly into your subconscious mind. And as I said, the repetitive negative information forms destructive beliefs. Where do you get this information? From media, TV, and the Internet, especially social media. Let's say you love to watch a show on TV about an abusive relationship. You are unconsciously programming your subconscious mind to experience what you watch on TV, especially if you are emotionally involved in what you love to watch. When you watch a show, and there is misbehavior in a relationship, your subconscious mind indirectly receives a message that the world is not safe to trust anyone in a deep, meaningful relationship. Then you start to think that way, and the world begins to confirm your thoughts.

You enter a relationship, the other person misbehaves, and you begin to judge him based on the information you already have in your subconscious mind. You blame the person with whom you are in a relationship and register your experience as strong evidence to confirm your core beliefs about relationships. The point is that data is powerful, and repetitive information entering the subconscious mind can create new feelings that induce new behavior.

The mind always looks for evidence to confirm its belief system. Children who grow up in divorced families are more likely to divorce later in life because children often observe their parents' behavior with each other as evidence of how a relationship should be. The quality of parents' relationships creates the children's belief system through which they perceive relationships. Later in life, their perception of relationships with siblings, family, and friends also impacts their belief system about how one can experience relationships. If the mind absorbs the negative information about relationships, it means that the belief system has a negative attitude toward relationships.

For example, someone talking for hours with a friend about her break up and arguing that "it is hard to trust anyone" forms a belief that a quality relationship is impossible. Or she may simply have had one or a few low-quality relationship experiences and concluded, through mental generalization, that there are not good people out there for a meaningful relationship. These perceptions, which are according to the core beliefs, imply unlovability, unworthiness, and incompetency for establishing a quality relationship. If you are already in a relationship, these negative perceptions about love hinder the growth of your relationship and the emotional evolution of love.

Use Your Will to Reject Negative Information about Relationships

Another example of how environmental information shapes our belief about relationships is when you read in books and journals or hear from experts on TV or the Internet that around 50 percent of relationships end in divorce. That is undoubtedly a high rate. The conscious mind evaluates the statistics regarding relationships and divorce rates in the following way: the statistics indirectly imply a strong message to the subconscious mind that there is a 50 percent chance that your current or future relationship will end by divorce. So, depending on how strong your constructive beliefs are regarding relationships, you can reject the negative information and maintain and even deepen your relationship.

The will faculty of the conscious mind is a tool that enables humans to accept or reject information they receive. It is naive to accept any information we hear that can be harmful. You can simply say to yourself, "I am going to be one of those who are experiencing a loving relationship," rejecting to be one of those in the 50 percent divorce rate. A wise way to use the will faculty is to accept the positive information and reject the negative. Again, it doesn't mean being naive and denying facts. A relationship shouldn't be left to statistics and chance, but it requires developing humanity, mutual understanding, patience, compromise, compassion, kindness, respect, and commitment.

Someone else's reality shouldn't become your reality. The external life reflects the inner world. Using the will faculty of the conscious mind enables you to reject negative information entering your subconscious mind and shaping your perception of relationships. The will faculty is a tool by which a human can practice free will. Apply your will faculty of the conscious mind to reject any negative information that wavers your hopes and constructive beliefs about a loving relationship.

Believe You Deserve Love

No one is perfect because perfection doesn't exist. Even in the best and most loving family environment, there are imperfections in the environment that would negatively affect kids who are highly sensitive and suggestible.

A fundamental requirement to experience love is to accept yourself as you are and deeply believe you deserve love, despite your past experiences. Humans are the only creatures that identify themselves as "I" and give some value to this "I" based on the norms and standards of society; hence, they disassociate themselves from one another, causing separation. But you should know that your true essence is love. Your true essence is life because when you were born, you were pure love and life. You are still the same pure love if you let what has been imposed on you through the environment, including family, friends, teachers, media, and so on, fall apart from your being. So claim love because your true essence is love, and you deserve it. Love is inside you. It is easy to be malleable when confronting external influences, but you can reject what external influences impose on you and choose love.

I accept that it is not easy work, but I assure you that very deep inside you is love, and your job is to uncover your treasure that might have been buried by others' mistreating you.

So, the first step in experiencing true love in a relationship is to firmly believe that love is real and that you deserve it.

You deserve love despite your social status, race, income, physical fitness, appearance, educational level, achievements, etc. And if you think otherwise, your perception about yourself is external programming imposed on you by the environment in which you have grown up; this programming gives value to your "I" based on what others have told you, whereas you deserve love independent of any external factors. Note that today's societies have many more influences on humans than before through the Internet and satellite media. Now, humans are programmed not only by the environment in which they grow up but also by global influences they can access through the Internet.

When you unbury your inner love, you become a source of love who can activate the dormant love in others. Love originates from your inner world and is infinite. There is no scarcity of love, as true love is infinite. The more you give love, the more you receive it. This is the art of loving in a relationship: to bring more love into the world, activate the dormant love in your partner, and help him connect to the true essence of love.

Evolving Self-Image and Partner-Image

The information we have received from the environment throughout childhood and life experiences shape our perception of ourselves. This perception is based on the mind's creation of an image of *self*, which is called *self-image*. The self-image forms your belief about who you are. Does your self-image perceive you as lovely, worthy, and competent? You are how you perceive yourself to be. If you improve your self-image through self-discovery, contemplation, and constructive beliefs, you can enhance your quality of life, including your relationship.

The first impression of your partner made a foundation for your *partner-image* in your mind. You begin to build an image in your mind about your partner the moment you first meet each other. Your partner-image updates by getting more information about your partner through interactions, talking, nonverbal communication, knowing your partner's family and friends, her fears and hopes, personality, and character. If your partner-image in your mind perceives your partner as worthy, lovable, and competent, you treat your partner based on the image you have built of your partner in your mind with love and respect. When you treat your partner with respect and honor, you express the partner-image in your mind. You perceive your partner as someone who deserves respect and love and behave accordingly.

In a loving relationship, your partner-image in your mind should improve, not deteriorate. You should create a beautiful image of your partner in your mind and keep that image until you see how your partner responds according to the image you have built of her in your mind.

You may say, "I have updated my partner-image in my mind based on facts I know now." However, these facts will not serve you for experiencing a loving relationship. You should continuously look for the positive aspects of your partner's personality, character, and capabilities and improve your partner-image in your mind. People often behave according to the image we make of them in our mind. Don't let thinking errors and maladaptive mental schemas distort your partner-image in your mind. (You will learn about thinking errors and cognitive schemas in Chapter 4 and Chapter 5, respectively).

What Story Are You Telling Yourself about Love?

Humans talk to themselves more than talking to anyone else in the world. Talking to the *self* is a mental activity. The story you tell yourself about anything in life reflects your belief about that thing, creating your personal reality. Likewise, the story you tell yourself about love is rooted in your childhood connection with your parents or primary caregivers and with others throughout your life. All your connections with people during your lifetime have been saved in your subconscious mind and are permanent memories. Your relationship experiences have become a reliable reference for your judgment to predict your future relationships and perceive how relationships among humans are. Mental models for relationships are saved in long-term memory. Long-term memory is categorized into implicit or explicit memories. Implicit memory is in the subconscious mind, and humans cannot remember it; however, the mind uses it to run body and mind functions.

On the other hand, humans consciously recall explicit memory, like when they want to remember a past event. For connection with your partner, your mind uses implicit memory, which you cannot recall or have access to, and it is running automatically. The story you tell yourself about your relationship wants to make sense of your implicit memory, which is functioning and creating your current relationship.

What are you telling yourself about relationships in general? Is love real? Based on the statistics, is divorce a high possibility in relationships, and might that experience happen to you? What does your relationship mean to you? What are the possibilities in your relationship?

If you perceive your relationship in a way that makes you feel hopeless, fearful, worried, or ambivalent, you should think about what you tell yourself. The story you tell yourself reflects on your relationship, and you project your inner world onto your partner.

Your relationship can grow and gradually be filled with love and passion. You should write a beautiful story about how you want your relationship to be and tell that story to yourself every day. Believe that it is possible to experience a more loving, passionate relationship and feel its fulfillment as you read your new story. By doing so, you detach yourself from your implicit memory that is running and shaping your relationship, and you begin to reprogram your subconscious mind to work with your new information to manifest your new story.

You don't need to be a prisoner of your past relational experiences; you can begin to create new memories so that your mental model for relationships and connections gets an advanced update. The story that we tell ourselves creates our feelings and personal reality. You may need to tell yourself a new story about your thriving relationship for at least a few months to create new neural pathways and circuits in your brain through which your mental energy flows smoothly without your conscious mind's effort so that the new story creates your new feelings to experience a quality relationship. It is easy for the mind to continue to work based on old programming. In your current mental model for connection, all the neural pathways and circuits are already ingrained, and the flow of mental energy passes smoothly, but you will get the same results in your relationship; the price for comfort and ease is to get the same results in your relationship. So, you should deliberately change the direction of your mental energy toward creating a new story for your relationship, which requires certainty, planning, effort, determination, and consistency.

Have a Vision for Your Love Relationship

The human mind is a goal-oriented system and works toward a well-defined goal. The goal should be clear and specific. Having a vague goal or multiple goals means having no goal in life. Concerning relationships, you should know where you are and where you are going. Your relationship vision helps your mind be on track and constantly move you forward to fulfilling your perspective of how you want your relationship to become. What does an ideal relationship look like for you? What do you yearn most to have in your relationship? One of the best ways to remind your mind of what you want and are looking for is to write about your ideal relationship and read it daily.

The mind is forgetful and needs to be reminded of what is important to work on. When writing about your ideal relationship, use your imagination and write beyond logical thinking. There is no limitation in the imaginary world. Imagination is one of the most powerful mental tools to use in the brain's right hemisphere. Any invention that has changed the world has been started in imagination. Studies have shown that practicing a new skill through imagination creates new neural pathways in the brain similar to those created by actually practicing the skill. Writing is a powerful tool for stimulating thinking and helps with clear thinking and focus. Begin to write about your relationship vision.

What does it look like?
What activities do you do with your partner?
How do you spend your time together?
How do you treat each other?
How sensitive and considerate is your partner toward your needs?
Where do you live together?
How does your partner appreciate and admire you?
What do you do together for fun?
Where will you travel together?
What would you like to hear often from your partner?
How exciting is your relationship?
How understanding is your partner?

How do you feel receiving your partner's love and affection?
How is your financial situation?
What does your sex life look like?

Read your vision script every day to remind yourself what you want. Set a goal aligned with the most important part of your vision. For example, let's say you want a lot more romance and quality time, which is the number one goal in your vision script for your relationship. Now, you should answer the following questions to clarify your goal:

What does romance mean to you?
What does romance mean to your partner?
What routine can you institute in your relationship that fosters romance and intimacy between you?

Set a forty-day timeframe to take action every day to achieve your desired goal in your relationship and build a new routine that brings more romance and intimacy. Remember that nothing changes in life unless we change our thoughts and perceptions and do something different; remember that change should occur gradually by continuous, small steps. What you are experiencing in your relationship is the fruit of years of programming from when you were born and developed your attachment mental model. So, changing your current intimate relationship to a more loving connection with your partner and developing a higher level of relationship requires a systematic plan, patience, hope, commitment, and consistency in taking action. Believe that having a dreamy relationship with your current partner is possible, but remember, it will not happen overnight. I assure you that when you start to work on yourself, continue on the growth path, and keep your hope alive, even when things get tough and seem gloomy, you will get what you seek. No attempt in the world is in vain. You may not see the result according to your timing, but sooner or later, you will see the positive effect of your attempts in your life. A voice inside your mind may say, “It’s not possible” or “It’s not going to work,” or similar words, conveying hopelessness and helplessness. *Do not listen to that voice.* You may need to read this section of the book many times to diminish the demoralizing voice inside you that comes from your attachment programming. The good news is that the more you feed your soul with positivity and empowering information, the more you believe that “It is possible” and that “It is going to work.” Notice small, positive changes in your relationship, cherish and acknowledge it, feel and express gratitude for it, and continue your path toward a more loving, fulfilling relationship.

Love and Sex

From a biological standpoint, sex is a reproduction mechanism. However, in a loving relationship, sex is the expression of love in its most physical and emotional closeness possible. Sex is a complex psychological, physiological, and spiritual process through which two humans express their deepest emotions and needs. Love should be an opening to a relationship, and when trust is built, sex follows. When you trust your partner, you share your fantasies about sex and are sure that your partner won't judge you or think less of you while you respect your boundaries in sex.

Love wants to be expressed, and sex is one of the strongest ways through which the energies of two humans are exchanged. The quality of sex positively contributes to the quality of a relationship; it is possible for a couple to have good sex even if their relationship is in trouble.

You should trust each other and talk openly and gently about sex. Try to know what your partner wants in sex and what you can do before, during, and after lovemaking. For women especially, it is essential that they feel safe and emotionally ready for intimacy. Men should spend more time on foreplay, avoid rapid sex, and wait until women are ready for intercourse. Unrealistic expectations of sex performance formed based on porn products can tremendously hurt men's self-confidence, resulting in sexual dysfunction.

Women need to be emotionally ready, be at peace, and feel safe before having sex with their man. If they are not ready for sex, they might refuse to have sex with their man, but that doesn't mean rejection. Men should understand and respect their women's emotional needs, express empathy, and provide emotional support rather than perceive their woman's refusal as rejection and humiliation. Household chores done by men are very erotic for women; studies show that when household chores are shared between couples in a way that is perceived as adequate and enough by women, it increases marriage and sex satisfaction. Men often overestimate their contribution to housework; men should know that contributing genuinely to housework can reduce the workload from women's shoulders and bring more peace to them, which eventually prepares women to have sex with their man.

Commitment Begins in Your Mind

Loyalty and commitment go hand in hand in a relationship. If you cherish and want a committed relationship, you should know that commitment in a relationship is not a one-time convention; it is a decision to commit at every moment and requires loyalty in your mind and actions. No matter how much you love and are attracted to your partner, there will be moments when you find someone else very attractive. And everything begins first in your mind, where your partner and others won't see. Then you have the choice to direct your attention toward your partner and remind yourself how much you love her and are committed, or you can let your mind direct your attention to make you fond of another person and fantasize being with that person; even though your partner doesn't know, you are not committed in your mind anymore. That might not be a dealbreaker, but it prevents your heart from evolving in love with your partner. I understand it is difficult to be loyal, especially at the mind level. However, a true commitment begins in your mind, and it is a sign of pure love in the relationship. Humans are complicated creatures, and they communicate with one another through languages and their emitted energy, reflecting the vibrations of their thoughts and feelings. Your partner may not consciously be aware of disloyalty in your mind. Still, the thoughts and energy of disloyalty communicate with your partner's energy, affecting your relationship.

The concept of loyalty and commitment in your relationship should be ingrained at a subconscious level so that at every moment, you unconsciously decide to be loyal to your partner. It is a challenge nowadays to stay committed and faithful in one's mind, as the hot topic in many serials, shows, and movies is cheating on a partner. When the mind receives a huge amount of data about cheating, it is hard to harness the mind and mentally stay loyal and committed. But the reward for being mentally and physically committed to your relationship is an opening to experiencing true love with your partner.

Look for Role Models Whose True Love Is Inspiring

Our perception of relationships is influenced by the quality of people's relationships around us, including parents, family, friends, neighbors, colleagues, and so on. Every relationship we know about is registered in the subconscious mind and used as a reference for our judgment and perception of relationships.

If you want to experience a loving relationship, a wise way to do so is to deliberately choose role models that are great examples of loving relationships. Choose one or more role models who inspire you on how a loving relationship can be and should be. You should consciously direct your thoughts toward your role models' relationships and the quality of their lives, feeling appreciation and admiration for what they have created. If you see many dysfunctional relationships around you, you should ignore them and pay attention to your role models' relationships.

You should *convince* yourself that a loving relationship is possible and refer to your role models' relationships as evidence to develop a positive belief about relationships. You should often talk to yourself about your role models' traits and behaviors concerning their relationships. Recognition of loving relationships, talking about those relationships, and appreciation and admiration for the people involved in creating those relationships should become one of your daily mental activities. A loving relationship is created from the inside out.

Write down below the key points you learned in Chapter 2.

Chapter 3

The Attachment Theory and Connection Styles

Attachment Theory and Love

Attachment theory was introduced first by John Bowlby, a British psychologist, in London, U.K., in the 1960s. The theory studies the development of attachment styles in children. Later, the theory expanded and also covered attachment styles in adulthood relationships.

When a newborn comes into this world, she is a pure subconscious mind and spiritual being connected directly to the Infinite Love. Then, she absorbs information from the environment, and by age two, her personality and character form. Her quality of connection with her primary caregivers shapes her connection style with other humans. She forms a secure attachment style if she is in a secure relationship with her caregivers and her needs have been fulfilled properly. She learns that, at the subconscious level, the world is a safe place, and she can trust others to fulfill her emotional and physical needs. If her primary caregivers have been partially available and the child has been always or sometimes neglected, physically or emotionally, then the child develops two different mechanisms to help her survive, and she forms an insecure attachment style.

One strategy to survive in an insecure environment is to cling to anyone available by developing an anxious attachment style. By doing so, the child perceives anyone reachable as a castle of refuge. Later in life, this connection-style programming is carried to adulthood and is expressed in connection with others. People with an anxious attachment style are preoccupied with their relationship and emotionally become dependent on their partner. They are sensitive and quickly fall in love.

Another strategy for a child growing up in an insecure environment is to become emotionally independent and distant from others. The child learns that the world is not somewhere you can rely on others. This strategy is called avoidant attachment style. For people with avoidant attachment style, being independent is highly valued, and any emotional and even physical closeness is unconsciously perceived as a threat. A person with an avoidant attachment style might want a quality relationship at the conscious level, but there is resistance to emotional closeness in the subconscious mind. It is like there is an inner wall for emotional protection. The subconscious mind always finds different ways to prevent any intimate relationship and is very good at doing it. One strategy the subconscious mind uses to avoid or end an intimate relationship is to find faults in the partner and magnify those faults. It also perceives good qualities in the self and exaggerates them to feel superior so that it has excuses to leave the relationship or keep emotional distance. People with an avoidant attachment style are usually alone and stay in the dating pool for a long time. And even if they enter a long-term relationship, they always keep some emotional distance and try to escape commitment.

Some people develop a mixed attachment style, combining both the anxious and avoidant styles and alternating between the two based on their surrounding circumstances. Studies show that about 48 percent of people are in their relationships with an insecure attachment style: either anxious, avoidant, or anxious-avoidant.

The good news is that about 52 percent of the population has a secure attachment style. People with a secure attachment style usually have grown up in an emotionally secure family with a stable, reasonably safe environment. Their adulthood experience also has been safe. They commit to a relationship and are not afraid of closeness. People with a secure attachment style are more susceptible to experiencing true love because of how they think, perceive, and behave in a relationship.

Oddly, people with anxious attachment style are usually attracted to people with avoidant attachment style. According to the attachment theory, this is because a relationship between someone with an anxious attachment style and one with an avoidant attachment style makes the anxious person excited and apprehensive, which is a familiar feeling for her. On the other hand, people with an avoidant attachment style, who are exposed to someone clinging in the relationship, make their emotional wall stronger to reinforce their emotional resilience and independence that they highly value. But this subconscious mind game emotionally damages both sides. The emotional needs of the person with an anxious attachment style won't be fulfilled, and the person with an avoidant attachment style won't experience true love and emotional closeness. Someone with an anxious attachment style often says something like, "I was fond of his independence and self-sufficiency" or "She was emotionally strong and autonomous; she didn't need anyone to help her." Because of a lack of self-awareness, avoidantly attached people often don't feel the need to change and don't know that the suffering of their inner world and relationship turmoil is due to their connection model defect; they usually go to a couples therapist at the insistence of their overwhelmed spouse who has an anxious attachment style.

Here is valuable advice to those with an anxious attachment style: Do not let emotional unavailability turn on your attachment style, the feeling of neediness, and emotional clinginess. *Do not let emotional unavailability make you fall in love.* When looking for someone to date, find out whether the person has signs of a secure attachment style, respects your feelings, and cares about your well-being.

Safety and Trust Required for Human Connections

People want safety before anything else, even food. Without safety, survival is threatened. The fear mechanism in the subconscious mind acts for the safety and continuity of life; it warns humans of danger, and through chemical reactions and hormonal release, it makes the body fight or fly in a fraction of a second. The fear mechanism has served humans for a long time and has been effective in the survival of the human species. But the fear mechanism also works as an emotional protective mechanism to defend against emotional breakouts.

In psychology, a fear underlies every human wish, hindering that wish from coming true. And those who overcome their fear will fulfill their wish. Physical and emotional safety and trust are pillars of a loving, lasting relationship. But one should overcome the fear of closeness and vulnerability. Human psychology is complex; sometimes, when you get close to someone, while you enjoy it, part of you may experience fear or doubt whether you deserve this level of closeness and intimacy. This is because, based on your attachment style, your subconscious mind interprets emotional closeness and vulnerability as a threat to emotional protection (avoidant attachment style). Or maybe you unconsciously have a strange feeling because you were neglected during your childhood and are unfamiliar with the feelings of closeness and intimacy (anxious-avoidant attachment style). If this happens to you, you should frequently remind yourself that you deserve love and a quality relationship. Love is already within you, and you are on the path to discovering your love, which has been buried inside you. Use sound reasoning and talk to yourself to convince yourself that you are worthy of love and that you deserve a quality relationship.

However, you should know that passing the emotional safety zone and trusting others is part of the human experience. You are responsible for setting a standard in your relationships and entering one based on love and respect. You should be willing to be vulnerable and trust others to come out of the *self* and become *one* with another human, creating the concept of *oneness* together. There is a cost to entering the path of love, and that is to overcome your fear of closeness and trust the right person based on your standard.

Clinging Is Not True Love

People with anxious attachment style have an ambivalent character and tend to cling to their partner in their relationship, thinking it is love. However, attachment theory explains that because of unmet emotional needs and uncertainty in receiving love and attention, the attachment system in those with anxious attachment style is activated and stays active until it gets a response from the person they are in a relationship with; then they feel gratified and relieved because they are temporarily reassured that the connection is still established. In a loving relationship, you should give your beloved freedom and space. Your partner's interests and emotional well-being are your interests and emotional well-being.

People with an anxious attachment style quickly fall in love, and they engage in the thinking error of positive mental filtering, seeing only the positives of the one with whom they have fallen in love; they have grown up in a family where a secure connection model has not been structured in the process of their mental development. They are unsure deep inside whether the connection they've built will last, which makes them anxious and thus unconsciously use the clinging strategy to keep the connection active in any way.

Ironically, the more that people with anxious attachment style cling to someone, the more that person will run away because he feels that his freedom is ignored and his emotional needs are compromised. As I talked about true love, the perception of true love is "What can I *give* in my relationship?" while someone with an anxious attachment style clings to a relationship and says, "What can I *get* in my relationship?" The attention focus of a person with an anxious attachment style is self-interest to fulfill unmet connection needs and temporarily soothe the wounds from childhood. I don't want to condemn such an expectation in a relationship; however, true love is far from clinging; it should expand from *self* and become bigger from within, giving without expectations and loving without conditions. Every experience in life has a lesson for us, and connection with others and relationships have a bigger purpose. If you feel that you cling to your partner, this is a good consciousness about your mental model of connection. Your partner is like a mirror showing your inner world. You should uncover your old programming and find out within yourself the Infinite Love from which you came on this planet. You should begin to practice self-love and self-compassion. You should perceive yourself as being worthy and lovable. And when you begin to connect within yourself and give yourself the love you deserve, you experience love in your external world through others. The solution to establishing a loving connection is not to cling but to develop self-love and self-compassion and be in harmony within the *self*.

The Power of Your Brain: A Priceless Asset

The brain is the hardware of the body's operating system. A brain has about one hundred billion neurons, each of which can connect to ten thousand neurons. When a neuron connects to another neuron, they form a synapse. The possibility of synapse connections in the brain is an astonishing number of ten raised to the power of one million. This means neurons can connect to each other in infinite ways. But your old programming uses a fraction of this power to operate your body and mental processes, including your attachment style, which is activated automatically in your subconscious mind when you want to connect with others. In addition, scientists have found that, despite the old belief that the brain wired during childhood is fixed and unchangeable, the brain has the neuroplastic ability by which it can rewire neural networks and change to create new circuits based on new experiences during its lifetime and adapt to the environment. The development of the brain and mind is an "experience-dependent" process through which new experiences influence the formation of neural networks in the brain. When a new experience is repeated enough, the new neural networks become permanent, and a new habit forms. To develop the art of a loving relationship, you should practice certain behaviors that will contribute the most to your relationship's flourishing. You have access to your powerful brain and mind to create new neural circuits and update your programming to experience a more fulfilling life. You should develop your mind through new experiences and practices. When you want to learn how to paint, you don't just read about painting; you should actively practice painting. You will never know how to paint beautifully by merely reading about painting. The same is true about developing the art of a loving relationship; you should practice a certain loving attitude to become good and even excellent in loving. No matter what your attachment style is and how your past experiences have been, your current love relationship shouldn't be the repetition of your past relationships.

Be Willing to Change to Develop a Secure, Healthy Attachment Style

As I mentioned earlier, children growing up in a family where their primary caregivers have been responsive to their emotional, psychological, and physical needs develop a secure mental model through which they perceive and expect to receive emotional care and attuned attention from those they interact with; they develop a secure attachment style and are often emotionally intelligent and responsive to the needs of their partner.

People with avoidant and anxious attachment styles should deliberately choose to date and build long-term relationships with those with a healthy, secure attachment style. They should be willing to move out of their comfort zone to gradually change their attachment style toward a healthy, secure attachment model.

The first step for a person with an avoidant attachment style is to develop the capacity to emotionally trust another human and be open to receiving love. Self-awareness is the first big step for change and growth. If you feel that you have an avoidant attachment style, don't blame yourself, your parents, your primary caregivers, or others. Accept who you are and decide to change to be more trusting and open to love and compassion. If someone gives you a gift, feel good about it and incorporate it positively by genuinely saying how kind the gift giver is to acknowledge her pure intention. Don't interpret it negatively, such as saying, "What does she want from me?"

People with anxious attachment style should also deliberately choose to date and build a long-term relationship with those with a secure attachment model. An emotionally intelligent partner is someone who can be responsive to your emotional needs. You can also work on your personal development and develop the concept of self-love and self-respect so that you feel you deserve love and respect. No matter how attractive a person is, if you have realized that person does not give you his emotionally attuned attention, you do not need to continue dating him. Remember that plenty of people have a secure, healthy attachment style and are responsive to your emotional needs.

The human brain is extremely powerful. There are infinite possibilities for attachment styles, and yours is only one of these. Even though we have categorized attachment styles into a few main categories, there are not two people with exactly the same attachment style. Everyone is different and unique and has grown up in a different environment. You can now choose to gradually change your attachment style to experience a more beautiful and meaningful relationship. You can change your attachment model.

Amelia has been in a relationship with Henry for about six months. When Henry talks about his future life and goals, he never mentions or involves Amelia in his plans to imply the possibility of having a future together. Amelia feels that Henry doesn't see her as a serious partner. She needs reassurance about the relationship, but she is not able to share her vulnerability with Henry. She doesn't feel emotionally safe, is full of self-doubt, and feels inferior. But she doesn't share her feelings with Henry because she fears she might seem too needy and lose him forever. She is afraid of rejection. So, she decides to reject Henry before he rejects her so their separation will be less painful. She stops communicating with Henry despite his attempts. Henry doesn't understand why Amelia has left the relationship.

Amelia has an anxious attachment style. She should know that genuine communication (explained in Chapter 7) would help her express her hopes and expectations in their relationship so that Henry would better understand how his treatment of Amelia looks to her. Had Henry cared for Amelia's concerns and been responsive to her emotional needs, Amelia could have continued her relationship with Henry and didn't need to leave Henry without explaining the cause of leaving.

Override Your Old Relationship Programming

In the first place, accept and take responsibility for everything happening in your life, including loneliness or an unsatisfactory relationship. Though in an abusive relationship, the best option would be to leave, in most unsatisfactory relationships, the solution is not to change your partner. This has happened over and over again, as couples therapists have mentioned: You may change your partner, but soon you face the same issues that you had with your previous partner, as if he is the same person with a different name and look. It is because life experiences are from the inside out, and we project our mind's programming onto the outside world. Life experiences and challenges are repeated until we learn their lessons.

People come into our life to show us our inner world and where we should work within ourselves to grow in life and humanity. It is not easy work because easy work is done by the subconscious mind, which is automatic and consumes minimal mental energy. Changing the subconscious mind's programming requires self-discovery, discipline, patience, emotional maturity, and the willingness to grow personally and spiritually.

Upgrading the Old Attachment Style

Bob's wife often complains and says frequently that she doesn't feel loved by him. After reading a few books on relationships, Bob is now aware that he has an avoidant attachment style. Though he feels love for his wife, he has barely said "I love you" to his wife during the ten years of their marriage. He is just not comfortable expressing his emotions. Now, he is determined to change and create new neural pathways in his brain. He has learned about neuroplasticity and wants to update his attachment style. He knows that it will be uncomfortable at the beginning, but the more he practices, the easier it will become for him to express his emotions and open up to his wife. He has firmly decided to tell his wife, "I love you," three times daily for forty days. He sets a date to begin his practice and uses affirmations to be ready to go beyond his comfort zone. Every time Bob says to his wife, "I love you," he frees himself from the old programming and reinforces the new neural pathways in his brain to create new neural circuits through which mental energy flows easily and permanently. When the new neural pathways and circuits become fixed in Bob's brain, saying "I love you" will be a new comfort zone for Bob, and he can express his love to his wife without feeling uncomfortable or annoyed. Bob is becoming comfortable with closeness and developing a secondary secure attachment style. Note that the first step for Bob to develop a secure attachment with his wife was self-awareness. He noticed that his mental model for connection with his wife had built a wall around his heart. He finally turned inward to find a solution when his wife rebuked him. He accepted his share in their conflicts. Bob was humble enough to take responsibility for their distant relationship and did not let his *ego* ignore the issue and blame others. He did not resist change but took a firm decision to express his love to his wife.

How Pain-Pleasure Principle Can Help People with Anxious Attachment Style

People with an anxious attachment style are more likely to be trapped in an abusive relationship. They become emotionally dependent by clinging to their partner. At the conscious level, they are aware that the relationship is abusive. Still, at the subconscious level, which rules their emotions and actions, they don't do anything about it and sometimes stay in a horrible relationship for years.

Maya has been in a relationship with George for eight years. George has been abusive and violent toward Maya many times. He doesn't respect her and talks in a way that implies his superiority to humiliate Maya. Nonetheless, Maya is emotionally attached to George and cannot leave him. Many of Maya's friends and her couples therapist have advised her to leave the relationship, but she simply can't bear emotional detachment from George.

Some critical factors explain why Maya cannot leave the relationship despite the relationship's abusiveness. Maya does not have a beautiful self-image. She doesn't perceive herself as someone who deserves love and respect and unconsciously doesn't expect love and respect from George. And humans receive what they expect to receive. She receives disrespect and violence from George, which confirms her self-image. Maya has learned about the pain-pleasure principle and wants to change her life and save herself from the abusive relationship.

Firstly, she wants to understand why she is staying in an abusive relationship. So she makes a table and writes down the gains and pains of being in the relationship with George.

Gains of Being in the Relationship	Pains of Being in the Relationship
• Emotional familiarity: 9 • Financial security: 8	• Disrespect: 5 • Violence: 5

Now, Maya can see that her gains from being in an abusive relationship (scored seventeen) are bigger than her pains (scored ten). Emotional familiarity has scored very high, indicating that Maya has an anxious attachment style. Because Maya has a poor self-image, the pain of disrespectfulness and violence each scored only five. Now she can see why she wants to stay in the relationship. Following the advice of her therapist, she decides to leave the relationship. As shown below, she modifies the pain-gain table so she can free herself from the abusive relationship.

Gains of Leaving the Relationship	Pains of Leaving the Relationship
• Learning self-love and self-respect: 5 • Leaving violence and disrespectfulness: 5 • Beginning a new, loving relationship: 6 • Financial independence: 8	• Emotional pain of leaving George: 9 • Facing with ambiguity: 5 • Financial challenge at the beginning of separation: 5

• Opening the art gallery with my sister: 7 • Doing activities that nourish my body and soul: 7	

Now Maya sees clearer and has more reasons why she needs to leave the abusive relationship with George. The gains of leaving the relationship scored thirty-eight compared to nineteen the score of pains of leaving the relationship. She has talked to her sister about moving to her sister's house when she leaves the relationship and will stay with her sister for a few months. She has read the pain-gain table of leaving the relationship for a few weeks and is now convinced that leaving the relationship with George is the best decision. She has developed more self-love and self-respect and feels she can't accept any more disrespectfulness and violence from anyone.

Write down below the key points you learned in Chapter 3.

Chapter 4

The Cognitive Behavioral Theory and Thinking Errors in Relationships

Cognitive behavioral theory (CBT) was first introduced by Dr. Beck in the 1960s. Cognitive simply means thinking. Studies show that just correcting the way of thinking in depressed patients treated more than 65 percent of people with severe depression in a relatively short period without taking any medications or other interventions.

When we talk about cognitive behavior, it means mental behavior; it is the mental behavior that creates different feelings and causes actions. A thought or collection of thoughts initiates mental behavior called a thought pattern. By changing your thoughts, you can change your mental behavior and, consequently, your feelings and actions.

The principle in cognitive behavioral theory is that any feeling is initiated by automatic thoughts, which are usually fleeting and unconscious. So, when a destructive feeling occurs in a relationship, a wise decision would be to find out the automatic thoughts behind that feeling and evaluate their trueness. Most of the time, we will see that the automatic thoughts, rooted in destructive beliefs about relationships, are distorted and far from the truth.

Cognitive Behavioral Awareness in a Loving Relationship

What you tell yourself creates your feelings. In a loving relationship, we should think properly and fairly, and cognitive behavioral awareness helps us think clearer. The mental attitudes are from the subconscious mind and are automatic. By learning about your thinking behaviors and evaluating their validity, you can better respond to the conflicts and incidents in your relationship. First, become aware of your feelings in a conflict. Then, try to detect your automatic thoughts behind your feelings and examine their validity using the ten *thinking errors criteria* explained later in this chapter. The more you practice detecting, writing down, evaluating, and rephrasing your distorted automatic thoughts, the better you become at controlling your emotions and solving conflicts in your relationship.

With patience and practice, you will be able to monitor your feelings and thoughts and choose thoughts that are closer to the facts and, therefore, truer. Distorted thoughts can be detrimental to a relationship. Cognitive behavioral theory is a scientifically proven way to understand mental behaviors better and constructively direct thoughts and emotions for well-being. One of the greatest discoveries in psychology and the principle of cognitive behavioral theory is that all emotions originate from thoughts; by altering our thoughts, we can change our emotions.

How Thinking Errors Hamper Loving Relationships

What is the benefit of the cognitive behavioral theory for a relationship? There are criteria in CBT that help detect *thinking errors* to prevent destructive feelings that ruin relationships. You should practice reflecting on your feelings and not let your subconscious mind drive you in your relationship. When you experience a negative feeling, there is something wrong that should be addressed. Negative feelings are not something to avoid but should be welcomed and taken care of. The problem with negative feelings is that when they stay with us for an extended period, we don't do anything to address the issue, and that causes dissatisfaction in relationships. Sometimes, addressing a negative feeling is as easy as applying genuine communication to eliminate misunderstanding.

When you sense a negative feeling about your partner or a situation related to your relationship, you should be patient before reacting, pause for a moment, and beware of what you are telling yourself. You should detect the automatic thoughts behind your feelings. According to Dr. Burns, a pioneer in CBT and the writer of the *Feeling Good* and *Feeling Great* books, there are ten criteria for distorted thoughts.

Do you remember the story of the loving couple I met in the Montreal metro station? His wife talked about patience being the secret of their fifty-four-year loving relationship. In developing the art of a loving relationship, you should be patient. One aspect of being patient is not reacting in undesired relationship incidents. Being patient is especially critical in using CBT to improve the quality of your relationship. If your partner behaves in a way that bothers you or an event makes you feel hopeless and frustrated, you should be patient and avoid the automatic reaction your mind has used so far. Instead, evaluate your thoughts to detect the automatic thoughts behind your negative feelings. Then, assess your thoughts and see which thinking errors you can detect in those thoughts patterns related to the situation. After, you can modify your thoughts and come up with ideas that are more accurate. Doing so lets you respond properly to the undesired partner's behavior or incident and positively control your emotions.

Note that when you use CBT, the aim is not to deny a fact but to think properly in a way that is closer to the fact. In the following, I introduce the ten *thinking errors criteria* that you may use to find distorted thoughts that cause relationship issues so that you can correct them.

1. All-or-Nothing Thinking

When you think about yourself, your partner, your environment, or your relationship in black and white, you put them in all-or-nothing categories. You don't see anything between the two extremes and don't pay attention to the gray in your partner and relationship.

Example: You wanted to go to a party, but your partner is late. You feel anxious and frustrated. You pause for a moment and detect the automatic thoughts behind your anxiety and frustration. You should always write down your automatic thoughts as soon as you detect them. You discern that you keep unconsciously repeating this statement to yourself: He is irresponsible and doesn't care about me and our relationship.

However, the thinking error of *all-or-nothing* makes this statement distorted and far from being true. If you evaluate your relationship, you will see that you can find situations and moments when your partner cared about you and your relationship and was responsible. So, it is fair to make your statement more specific and communicate with your partner when the situation is peaceful. Tell him that when he does so-and-so, it makes you feel uncared for and anxious.

2. Overgeneralization

When you perceive an event or situation as a never-ending incident, you have fallen into the mind trap of *overgeneralization*.

When you are rejected by someone you love, you might tell yourself, "I am unlovable and unwanted, and I will be alone forever." Notice that you have associated one event with your entire being and life forever. Overgeneralization is a thinking error, as it doesn't see many possible situations that may happen in the future. Furthermore, evidence shows that you are a lovely person; however, you overlook the evidence because of the thinking error of overgeneralization.

3. Mental Filter

It is a positive mental filter when you dwell on the positives in your relationship or partner and overlook the negatives. You only see the good things in your relationship and partner or the one you have fallen in love with. The positive mental filter corresponds with people with an anxious attachment style. They might have the thinking error of the positive mental filter to idealize the one with whom they have fallen in love and overlook the negatives. They might dwell on the positives of the person with whom they are in love to such an extent that they don't see their own worth and positives; therefore, they lose their self-esteem and feel inferior.

The negative mental filter is when you exclusively think about an issue in your relationship, become preoccupied with your partner's or your negative behavior, and ignore all the positive things in your relationship or partner. You may overthink an issue in your relationship or misbehavior by yourself or your partner. The negative mental filter can, by focusing on shortcomings and ignoring positive qualities and conditions, lower your self-esteem and cause anxiety and anger. The thinking error of negative mental filter corresponds with people with avoidant attachment style. When people with an avoidant attachment style date or are in a relationship, they use the negative mental filter to think exclusively about small imperfections in their partner. They might use their dislike of how their partner dresses, eats, or talks as an excuse not to become emotionally close. By using the negative mental filter, people with an avoidant attachment style keep an emotional distance from their partner and stay in their familiar feeling of lovelessness.

4. Discounting the Facts

Discounting or ignoring facts can negatively affect relationships. You have seen that people with an avoidant attachment style don't respect your feelings on dates; however, you keep dating those people. For example, someone you are dating is frequently mentally disengaged when you talk; nonetheless, you ignore the fact and continue to date the person, or you may be complimented for something you have done or your good qualities, but you tell yourself, "They want to make me feel good. That's the only reason they compliment me."

In another instance, a woman with an anxious attachment style is in a relationship with a man with an avoidant attachment style. The woman sees that the man flirts with another woman all the time; notwithstanding, she ignores the fact and stays in the relationship and does not ask his man to respect her feelings. She has fallen into the mind trap of *discounting the facts*. Note that the man with an avoidant attachment style uses flirting as a way to keep emotional distance from the woman with whom he is in a relationship.

5. Jumping to Conclusions

If you tend to jump to conclusions without sufficient facts and evidence, you should know that jumping to conclusions is a twisted thought. There are two main forms of the jumping-to-conclusions thinking error:

a. Mind Reading

If you make assumptions about how your partner or one you date feels and thinks, you may have fallen into the mind-reading trap. Though you might have a beautiful feeling toward your partner, you don't express your emotions because you think that expressing your emotions is too intimate while in reality, unconsciously, you want emotional distance to stay in your comfort zone of life without intimacy. Notwithstanding, you assume that your partner receives your love and attention without verifying it with her.

Another example is when telling yourself that your relationship is very good while it is not the same thing your partner thinks and feels. Genuine communication is crucial to avoid the thinking error of mind reading. Studies show that even those people who think they are very intuitive make mistakes most of the time when engaging in mind reading. So, don't fall into the mind-reading trap; communicate effectively with your partner to know what she thinks and how she feels, and be genuinely caring.

b. Fortune Telling

You predict the future, while in reality, no one knows what will happen in the future. You have been in a few relationships, but none have worked. You start to tell yourself, "I will never have a loving relationship." This statement is a thinking error as you predict your future, while in reality, the future is uncertain. The statement also implies that good people are scarce in the world, so it is not possible to begin a meaningful relationship with one of them. All of your evidence is a few failed relationships, and your future love life should not be the continuation of your past relationships. There are unlimited possibilities in the future, but you should detach yourself from the past to be ready to receive a loving relationship. People with an anxious attachment style should be aware of the fortune-telling thinking error and remind themselves that there are plenty of wonderful people in the world to date and love.

People with an avoidant attachment style, while rejecting those they date emotionally, predict that they will meet their special one in the future. As no one is perfect, they usually never meet the special one and stay alone. The thinking error of fortune-telling keeps them in their familiar feeling of being emotionally deprived.

6. Magnification and Minimization

You perceive things and circumstances out of proportion. You either magnify or minimize something's importance inappropriately. This thinking error is often used by people with an avoidant attachment style. The mind uses the magnification and minimization thinking error to minimize others' good qualities and magnify their flaws. You may see your partner as too needy, sensitive, or overreacting while your partner needs your love and care. A woman with an anxious attachment style unknowingly uses the magnification and minimization thinking error to minimize her partner's flaws while magnifying her partner's good characteristics.

7. Emotional Reasoning

You may say, "Come on! Many say, 'See how you feel and respect your feelings.'" Nevertheless, according to cognitive behavioral theory, thoughts generate feelings. So, if those thoughts are distorted, your feelings can be misleading and may not be a valid source for reasoning. Hence, emotional reasoning is a thinking error.

An example of an emotional-reasoning thinking error is when your partner doesn't come home as usual; you feel anxious and imagine that he is cheating on you. In reality, his car had broken down, and he had been fixing it for hours. In this example, the distorted thoughts and images of cheating were causing an invalid feeling of anxiety. The thought was far from being true but caused you to feel anxious and nervous. Your innocent partner was struggling to fix his car!

In another instance, you may feel alone and conclude that you are unsociable and can't connect with anyone, though you can learn and develop social skills and meet people who match your style. The emotional-reasoning thinking error in this instance is that you use your feelings as a valid source for your reasoning. When you conclude that "I am unsociable and cannot connect with anyone," you take no action and stay in your comfort zone of being alone and not connecting with others.

The emotional-reasoning thinking error usually begins with *I feel*. On a date, you meet someone and feel terrific, telling yourself, "I feel so excited and lucky; I've found the man (woman) of my dreams." You enter the relationship quickly, but later, you find yourself in a troubled relationship.

Nonetheless, if the thoughts behind your feelings are correct and close to the fact, your feelings are valid. You should always ask yourself, "What am I telling myself that I feel ...?" and evaluate the validity of your thoughts.

People with an avoidant attachment style may say, "I'm not ready to commit," even when they have been in a relationship for years. They say so because they listen to their familiar feeling of not committing. If they follow this feeling, they end up alone. Commitment is the price one should pay for a lasting, loving relationship.

Be aware that your mind might use different approaches to make you feel miserable. You may feel guilty as your mind uses the emotional-reasoning thinking error. You may implicitly tell yourself, "I feel guilty, so I am a bad person." These feelings come from distorted thoughts; some mistakes don't make a human entirely bad. So don't try to prove that you are wrong. Let the feeling of guilt go and be hopeful and positive about yourself and your relationship.

8. Should Statements

There are two categories of should-statements thinking error. Should statements are usually hidden and reflect your opinion about yourself, others, and the world. Should statements may contain shoulds, musts, oughts, or simply be hidden rules you have set upon yourself, others, or the world.

a. Self-Directed Shoulds

These should statements are rules that you have set upon yourself. If you violate any of these *shoulds*, you feel guilty, shameful, depressed, or worthless. For instance, when you date someone and say something that doesn't match your should statements, you tell yourself, "I shouldn't say that; I ruined everything; I'm so dumb." You feel guilty and worthless.

b. Other-Directed Shoulds

This form of should statements are your rules that others are obliged to follow; otherwise, you become frustrated and angry. You think you have a high moral standard and everyone should have the same moral standard. Other-Directed shoulds might cause conflicts in relationships because people's shoulds and shouldn'ts are not usually the same. If you fall into the other-directed shoulds thinking error, you expect your partner to follow the rules you have set based on your belief system.

9. Labeling

Labeling oneself or others is a thinking error and is a form of extreme overgeneralization because you view your entire being as worthless, unlovable, defective, incompetent, unsocial, or bad. People with an anxious attachment style might label themselves unattractive or undesirable. On the other hand, people with an avoidant attachment style might label themselves superior in a relationship. In reality, no one is entirely bad or entirely good.

10. Blame

If you scrutinize to find faults in yourself or others, you are engaging in the thinking error of self-blame or others' blame. People with an anxious attachment style find faults in themselves and so blame themselves in their relationships, while people with an avoidant attachment style scrutinize their partner to blame their partner's faults. When people blame their partner in a relationship, they feel innocent and overlook their contribution to the conflict. Blaming others is the easiest way for the ego not to take responsibility in a conflict.

When blaming others, there are advantages like feeling morally superior or feeling right without feeling guilty. You may backbite your partner with your family and friends; they might agree with you and make you feel relieved and acknowledged. Though blaming your partner might feel good and easy, it never helps you solve issues in your relationship, and you easily fall into the mind trap of blaming others. The best way is to blame no one and find the root causes of the problem in oneself. And that is not something the ego wants because the ego thinks it is perfect and does not need any change or improvement. Blaming oneself or your partner wastes mental energy that otherwise you could use to solve the conflict in your relationship and understand your deep, unmet needs and those of your partner. Stopping to blame oneself and others is the beginning of personal growth.

How to Use Thinking Errors Awareness to Improve Relationships

One of the pillars of a quality relationship is to be patient. When we face a conflict in a relationship, the automatic programming in the subconscious mind reacts. The reaction might be destructive based on what we have learned from family, friends, media, and our environment. We should learn to pause the reaction of the subconscious mind and evaluate the validity of the thoughts that have generated the feelings in the conflict. To do so, we should be patient.

Based on cognitive behavioral theory, the first step is to detect and write down the automatic thoughts behind your feelings in a relationship conflict. Then, you should detect the thinking errors I discussed earlier in this chapter. The automatic thoughts might have one or all of the thinking errors. Afterward, you should modify your thoughts to make them closer to the fact; thus, those thoughts become truer. You also record the intensity of your feelings from one to ten, with one being the lowest and ten being the highest intensity. This way, you can measure your feelings before and after modifying your thoughts.

To show how this method works, I will tell the story of Jessica and her husband, Ted. Jessica works from home. About eight months ago, Jessica was busy with some project at home and asked Ted to bring their kid, Mike, to the park so that she could focus on the project and finish her work. While Mike was playing with other kids, he fell from the slide and injured his feet badly, so they had to take Mike to the hospital. Even though Mike is fine now, Jessica cannot trust Mike anymore to go out with Ted without her, especially since she knows that Ted was talking with his friend when Mike fell from the slide. She feels very anxious when his husband goes out with Mike without her.

Here is how she detected her automatic thoughts causing her anxiety. She sat down, took a piece of paper, made a 4-column table, and wrote her feelings, their intensity, and the automatic thoughts behind those feelings, detecting the thinking errors associated with the distorted automatic thoughts, as shown in the following.

Feelings	Intensity	Automatic Thoughts	Thinking Errors
Anxiety	8	- Ted is a careless father. - I feel something bad is going to happen if Mike and his dad go out without me.	- Labeling - Jumping-to-Conclusions - Emotional reasoning - Negative mental filter - Overgeneralization
Guilt	7	- I shouldn't have let them go out last time that Mike was injured.	- Blaming - Should statements - Jumping-to-Conclusions

When Jessica's automatic thought tells her, "Ted is a careless father," she sees now that it is a distorted thought. The automatic thought labels Ted as a careless father, while many pieces of evidence show Ted is a loving, caring father. "Ted is a careless father" also has jumping-to-conclusions and negative mental filter thinking errors. Because of one incident, Jessica's automatic thought jumps to the conclusion by telling herself, "Ted is a careless father." Jessica's mind also filters all the evidence that proves Ted is a responsible and caring father and lets the memory of the accident run in her subconscious mind. Overgeneralization is another thinking error in the "Ted is a careless father" thought.

The automatic thought of "I feel something bad is going to happen if Mike and his dad go out without me" has at least three thinking errors: jumping-to-conclusions, emotional reasoning, and overgeneralization.

When Jessica's automatic thought tells her the mentioned statement, it jumps to the conclusion without considering facts and valid premises. She predicts an incident in the future that falls into the fortune-telling thinking error.

The statement begins with *I feel,* indicating it is an emotional-reasoning thinking error. The cause of anxiety is distorted thoughts, so the feelings cannot be a valid prediction reference. This statement also implies the overgeneralization thinking error, extending a one-time incident to all of Mike's future outdoor activities with his dad.

Jessica also feels guilty and responsible for what happened to their kid. The automatic thought of "I shouldn't have let them go outside last time that Mike was injured" induces Jessica to feel guilty and engages her in the thinking error of self-blaming. The automatic thought misdirected Jessica, so she jumped to the conclusion that she should have predicted the future and not let Mike go out with his dad so that she could prevent Mike's injury.

Now that Jessica has found the thinking errors in her automatic thoughts, she makes another table and modifies the automatic thoughts so that they are truer and closer to the facts.

Feelings	Intensity	Modification of the Automatic Thoughts
Anxiety	2	- Ted is a caring and responsible father. He does his best to protect Mike, and I have seen it many times. - No one can predict the future, so I stay in the present moment and trust everything will be fine.
Guilt	2	- I could never have predicted what would happen to Mike. I am a normal human and can't control everything in the outside world.

You can see that after Jessica modified her thoughts, the intensity of her anxiety and guilt tremendously reduced. She will read the new, modified thoughts a couple of times every day and when she feels anxious or guilty about what happened to Mike. Jessica is on the path to rebuilding trust with Ted.

Write down below the key points you learned in Chapter 4.

Chapter 5

The Schema Theory: Mental Behaviors in Relationships

We can find the root of many adult behaviors in childhood experiences. One of the psychology schools of thought is the schema theory, which was first introduced by Dr. Jeffrey E. Young. Schemas refer to the coping strategies that a kid develops to manage and adapt to the environment in which she is growing up. The schemas are thought patterns through which a child continues to perceive herself, connect or disconnect with the environment and other people, and interpret how the world works and how she should think and behave in life.

Emotional Deprivation: A Love Blockage

There are eighteen maladaptive schemas due to unmet needs during childhood that explain human behavior and mental patterns, among which is the *emotional deprivation* schema. Studies show that about 60 percent of the population endures some degree of emotional deprivation. The root of the emotional deprivation schema is receiving inadequate love and attention during childhood. A child growing up in an emotionally deprived environment does not become familiar with the feeling of love and closeness. When an emotionally deprived child grows up and wants to begin a close, loving relationship, at the subconscious level, he rejects the relationship because the unfamiliar feelings of love and emotional closeness are uncomfortable and somehow unknown. The subconscious mind uses different ways to end the relationship or keep the person in an emotionally unavailable relationship. Starting a relationship with someone in another city, town, or country and being attracted to married people or anyone who will keep the person in an emotionally deprived situation and who will be emotionally unavailable are signs of an emotionally deprived personality. Emotionally deprived people usually use two opposite approaches in a relationship, and both of them provide the same result: emotional unavailability of the person with whom they are in a relationship or someone to whom they are attracted.

Based on schema theory, one strategy is that they become anxious in the relationship and cling to the other person. They just want to give attention to their partner and don't want to receive love because they are unconsciously unfamiliar with love. The more they cling to their partner in a relationship, the more their partner runs away and keeps them in the familiar feeling of emotional deprivation.

The opposite strategy that emotionally deprived people may use in a relationship is to become emotionally cold toward their partner and build a wall around their heart. By doing so, they reject any feeling of love and keep themselves unconsciously in the familiar feeling of emotional deprivation.

It is highly possible that two people with emotional deprivation schema enter a relationship, and each uses one of the two mentioned strategies. In that case, one person in the relationship becomes so giving without the ability to receive, and the other person becomes emotionally cold and doesn't receive the love her partner is giving. Eventually, both of them end up being emotionally deprived, staying in their familiar feelings.

What Emotional Deprived People Can Do in a Relationship

If you feel you have some degree of the emotional deprivation schema, you can gradually change your habitual behavior in your relationship and introduce love to your being as a new, familiar feeling.

Self-awareness is 50 percent of the treatment for maladaptive mental schemas. When you understand why you behave in certain ways and find out the root causes of your conflicts in your relationship, the problem is halfway solved. If you feel it is difficult to receive love, firstly, be aware of your emotional resistance, acknowledge its existence, and gradually accept loving comments and gifts. Tell yourself, "I am lovable and worthy of love; I welcome love into my life." You should be patient, read, and tell yourself many times daily the above affirmation until you begin to accept the act of kindness that your partner does, acknowledge it, and express your genuine gratitude for your partner's love and attention; it requires your attention, discipline, and patience, but, eventually, you will become familiar with the feeling of love and openness.

Observe your thoughts and behaviors and find out what thoughts and behaviors your mind uses to reject receiving love and kindness. Acknowledge the love-preventive thoughts and behaviors, but don't judge or blame them, yourself, or others. Instead, think about ways you can become open to receiving love. Everyone is unique, so you should think about how you can receive love but not resist it.

If you use a clinging approach in your relationship and seem too needy, you should know that it is a subconscious mechanism to cope with emotional deprivation. In this situation, you only want to give to your partner and think that you don't need to receive anything in return. The best scenario is that you begin a long-term relationship with someone emotionally available and responsive to your emotional needs. You can start to develop self-acceptance and self-love. You should know that beyond all those emotional needs lies your true being: pure love. Let go of your poor self-image and see yourself as lovable and worthy. When you begin to view yourself as a lovely being and focus on your beauty, your inner feelings and your perception of yourself will reflect on your outer world, and your partner will treat you the same way you treat yourself. You receive love if you believe you are lovable. You receive respect if you believe you are worthy of respect.

Schema Theory and Attachment Theory

The schema and attachment theories are both valid and reputable schools of thought in psychology. They share similarities, and knowing about each helps better understand human mental patterns and behaviors. For example, emotional deprivation in the schema theory is similar to the anxious-avoidant attachment style in the attachment theory. Both theories are valuable knowledge resources for those who want to understand their inner world better and the root causes of their behavior.

In addition to the emotional deprivation schema mentioned before, I will now discuss some other schemas related to relationships. Please note that learning about the maladaptive schemas is for self-discovery and self-awareness. Don't blame yourself, your partner, or others if you find out you or your partner might have some maladaptive schema.

Abandonment or Instability Schema

This schema works as a part of the belief system. A person with an abandonment schema usually grew up in an unstable and chaotic family. The person has been programmed to believe and expect that a relationship doesn't last due to cheating, death, divorce, breakup, diminished passion, and so on. The person with an abandonment schema might be in constant feelings of worry and fear of losing his partner and their relationship. This person should become aware that he is running the program of his childhood and reacting unknowingly to the relationship with an outdated coping strategy. People with abandonment schema might need their partner to reassure them frequently about their relationship and love. A child growing up in a single-parent family might develop an abandonment schema. The key point is that your current or future relationship shouldn't be based on what you have been programmed during childhood. If you feel you have an abandonment schema, you can change it by building solid trust with your partner and frequently reminding yourself of role models who have loving, stable relationships.

Mistrust or Abuse Schema

Children growing up in an environment where they have been physically or emotionally abused develop the belief that the world is not a safe place and that others might seriously hurt them if they trust others. People with the thought patterns of mistrust or abuse schema perceive the world based on their childhood experiences and predict what would happen if they trust others:

- Others want to hurt them physically or emotionally
- Others might deceive them
- Others might lie to them

People with mistrust and abuse schema are more likely to have difficulty establishing social connections with others and beginning a relationship. The old programming of childhood, perceiving others as untrustworthy and unreliable, may affect relationships between couples. When you know the root causes of mistrust, you can update your programming and interact in the world with a more realistic approach.

Defectiveness or Shame Schema

Children who have not felt worthy and valued and have been exposed to humiliation and condemnation might develop the defectiveness or shame schema through which they perceive themselves as if something is wrong with them that makes them unlovable and thus unworthy of care and attention. The thought pattern of the defectiveness schema finds something physically, emotionally, or psychologically wrong in oneself. People with defectiveness schema may perceive themselves as ugly and physically unattractive and believe that they are not lovable and feel shameful. People with defectiveness schema have received demoralizing information during their childhood from the environment and have formed a poor self-image of themselves. They think others might view them the same way they perceive themselves. The defectiveness schema is not valid and is based on others' opinions when the person has been a child and extremely suggestible by external information. Developing self-love and self-compassion and cherishing one's beauty are excellent ways to relieve the defectiveness and shame schema.

How does the defectiveness schema hinder people from receiving the love they long for? People get what they expect to receive in life; if some people have a poor self-image, they tend to have a low standard in their relationship with their partner. Because of the thought patterns of defectiveness, they feel they are not worthy of love and attention.

Feeling something is wrong with you is most likely rooted in your childhood experiences with your parents, siblings, or classmates in school. To overcome the defectiveness schema, think about this: No one is flawless. Everybody has many good qualities and some flaws. Reevaluate yourself and find beauty in your personality, character, physical body, good traits, and constructive habits. Changing the solidified patterns of thought is not easy, but it is possible, and it may take a few months if you work on it every single day. You can write down the reasons proving why you are lovely and worthy of care and attention. You may feel uncomfortable writing the reasons; however, beware that it is not you who are uncomfortable; it is your old programming, the defectiveness schema, that is uncomfortable because changing you means the death of the maladaptive schema. After you write down the reasons, write a letter to yourself and explain why you are worthy of love and attention and deserve to have a loving relationship. Contemplate and reflect on your reasons and read your letter every day for at least three months or until you are convinced and feel you are worthy of love and attention, deserving a loving relationship.

Sometimes, the feeling of shame comes from the sense of guilt. All humans make mistakes; no one is immaculate, and by making mistakes, humans learn and grow. Self-forgiveness is a powerful way to release oneself from the mental patterns of shame and guilt.

Social Isolation and Alienation Schema

Having the social isolation schema means one feels he is not part of the society and is estranged. Thought patterns associated with social isolation and alienation schema, such as "I am very different from others" or "I am not part of the society," create feelings that hinder a person from effective social interactions and connection with others. The feeling of disconnectedness from others might persist in this schema even though the person might socially seem active. A person with social isolation and alienation schema feels that he is not accepted in the society where he belongs. This mental schema can keep one in isolation with minimal social connections, causing solitude or loneliness. The truth is that social interactions and integration are learnable skills, and, like any other skills, one can develop them.

Failure Schema

Failure schema creates a strong sense that one is a failure compared to others. A person with the failure schema believes that she has not been successful and is unable to be successful in some areas of life.

The failure schema can cause one with unsuccessful past relationships to perceive herself as a failure in relationships and believe that she cannot experience a loving, authentic relationship. The intense feeling of being a failure in a relationship causes the person not to expect a loving relationship and hinders the person from looking for a new partner.

Entitlement or Grandiosity Schema

People with an entitlement schema feel superior to others. They put their interests over others' and always want things done their way. They feel they are unique; they think they are better than others and deserve special recognition and privileges. The entitlement and grandiosity mental schema can cause emotional distance in a relationship and hinder the couple from building a loving connection based on respect and mutual interests. One with an entitlement or grandiosity schema has a big ego that prevents him from emotional closeness and *oneness* that both require a sense of unity and equality.

Emotional Inhibition Schema

People with an emotional inhibition schema suppress the expression of their emotions and are uncomfortable being exposed to others' expressions of emotions as well. They may be afraid that expressing emotions might hurt others' feelings, causing them shame or losing others' approval. In a relationship, inhibition of emotions can cause problems, preventing emotional closeness and inducing miscommunication. Establishing a safe environment and building a solidified trust can help a partner with an emotional inhibition schema express emotions and gradually develop a more constructive mental pattern.

Unrelenting Standards and Criticism Schema

An unrelenting standards schema creates the feeling of pressure on one to meet very high standards at work, business, or relationships. This schema can cause problems in relationships because the person might become too busy at work or on other projects to measure up to the unrelenting standards for those activities, so she can't pay attention to the relationship. In this mental schema, the feeling of "nothing is good enough" persists while the person strives hard to avoid inner criticism. Self-awareness about this schema and creating a good work-life balance can help harness the unrelenting standards schema.

Negativity or Pessimism Schema

People with the negativity or pessimism schema look for downsides to everything in life and expect undesired outcomes. They scrutinize their relationship to find flaws in their relationship or partner. The mental patterns associated with this schema perceive negativity in life. They are good at exaggerating negativity and flaws and discounting positivity and goodness. Training the mind can transform negativity and pessimistic mental patterns into optimistic ones, helping a relationship thrive.

Insufficient Self-Control or Self-Discipline

This mental schema makes accepting failure and setbacks intolerable. People with insufficient self-control or self-discipline are impatient and give up quickly with the slightest discomfort and difficulty on their path to achieving something. This maladaptive schema can cost a person in a relationship when he faces a conflict or setback regarding the relationship. People with this mental schema don't tolerate flaws or conflicts in their relationship, so they often end their relationship or avoid a new connection to prevent potential suffering from conflicts and disagreements in a relationship.

As I will discuss in the next chapter, conflicts are opportunities in a relationship to know yourself and your partner, practice compassion, learn how to compromise, become a problem solver, and develop self-confidence and self-esteem. The solution that the insufficient self-control or self-discipline schema gives you is to escape conflicts because facing them is painful whereas your growth is in being patient, accepting the initial pain caused by your old schema, and building up new mental patterns to solve problems in your relationship and become a better version of yourself.

Approval-Seeking Schema

People with approval-seeking schema excessively and constantly seek others' approval and recognition for what they do or how they look, depending on others' opinions for their self-worth. It is natural to want others' approval and recognition for what we do; however, when the desire for others' approval becomes the foundation of our inner world and self-worth, it becomes abnormal. The approval-seeking schema can hurt self-esteem by relying on external factors to feel worthy. Low self-esteem based on a lack of others' approval can adversely affect people when choosing a partner for a relationship. Your relationship is the reflection of your deep inner world, the way you perceive yourself. Your worthiness should erupt from within, and a nuanced balance between self-approval and others' recognition is the key to feeling adequate. When you are in a true, loving relationship, your partner will accept you for who you are, perceiving you as worthy and deserving of love while you also perceive yourself as worthy and deserving of love. Self-approval and self-recognition are the antidote to transforming the approval-seeking schema into constructive mental patterns to feel worthy, adequate, and lovable.

Write down below the key points you learned in Chapter 5.

Chapter 6

Conflicts in Relationships: Opportunities for Growth

Conflicts in Relationships

One of the biggest myths about relationships is that a great relationship is without conflicts. There will always be conflicts in a relationship, but how couples think and behave when facing those conflicts makes one relationship thrive and another decline. When a conflict is faced in a relationship, people with a loving attitude perceive it as an opportunity to express their true love through compromising, forgiving, respecting, caring, flexibility, and genuine communication. In a good relationship, conflicts are not problems but opportunities to grow and mature in love. When couples see conflicts as a problem in their relationship, they use them as excuses to create emotional distance, and this process often occurs at the subconscious level. An open-minded person will ask these questions when facing a conflict in a relationship:

What can I learn about my partner?
What can I learn about myself?
What opportunity exists in this conflict?
How can I lovingly respond to this conflict?
How can we solve this conflict so that we become even closer to each other?

The art of a loving relationship is to respond to conflicts lovingly and not let the programming of the subconscious mind automatically react to the conflict without considering the negative consequences. One of the devastating strategies for dealing with conflicts in relationships is to avoid or hide them. This strategy may work for a little while, but it will be detrimental to the relationship in the long term. Heated arguments and even grudges form when unresolved conflicts are hidden, avoided, or ignored by one or both people in the relationship.

Character and Personality Differences

Character and personality are two different human constituents. Personality is associated with more visible or noticeable human attributes such as being beautiful and tall (physical personality), having a sense of humor, having a lovely voice, and so on. On the other hand, character consists of inner attributes such as kindness, caring, compassion, understanding, honesty, loyalty, and so on. Personality is what people usually fall in love with because personality is visible and easy to recognize at the beginning of an acquaintance. Later, when they are in a relationship, they gradually get to know the character of their partner's inner world attributes. If the inner attributes of their partner, which were not visible or noticeable at the beginning of their relationship, don't meet their standard and expectations, they feel frustrated, overwhelmed, and sometimes angry. They feel like they have fallen into a trap because at first they were attracted to their partner's visible personality, but they now encounter their partner's undesired character. Mismatch of personality and character can cause conflicts in relationships. Nevertheless, what is vital in developing a lasting, loving relationship is accepting both the personality and character of your partner, the good attributes and the flaws.

A Loving Relationship Needs More than Just Great Chemistry

Chemistry is a great attraction factor at the beginning of a relationship. Visible aspects such as beauty, fitness, financial condition, social status, achievements, academic certificates, prestigious careers, and intellectual abilities are appealing and can create profound chemistry. However, compatibility is what keeps two people together in a long-term relationship.

The concept of "emotional intelligence" was introduced by Daniel Goleman and has been admired and considered since the publication of his book, "Emotional Intelligence: Why It Can Matter More than IQ." Emotional intelligence has five main components: self-awareness, self-management, motivation, empathy, and social skills. Emotionally intelligent people are aware of their feelings and needs; they know how to respect their feelings and express their needs effectively. They are good at managing their emotional frustration in a non-destructive way and calming themselves down when they are angry. Motivation in emotionally intelligent people is instinctive and internal, helping them to pursue their meaningful purpose in life and have a positive perspective about challenges and setbacks. Empathy means attentively listening to your partner and effectively communicating with her verbally or nonverbally to show that you understand and feel for your partner. Social skills help emotionally intelligent people to connect, interact, and work with others efficiently. Emotionally intelligent people demonstrate genuine empathy, caring, support, and compassion for their partner and other people in general. Emotional intelligence is a skill and is learnable.

In addition to emotional intelligence for a thriving, lasting relationship, spiritual compatibility is an important element. Spiritual compatibility is the harmony between two souls and the attunement of two states of mind. When you and your partner connect on a very deep level and bind your inner worlds with the bridge of love, you have spiritual compatibility.

Chemistry is not enough for a loving relationship. You should fall in love with the personality and character of your partner, meaning you should accept and appreciate both the visible attributes and inner traits of your partner. You want to connect with your partner intellectually, emotionally, and spiritually.

Have the Courage to Solve Conflicts

As I said, we should perceive conflicts in a relationship as opportunities for growth. People who run away from problems in life do not grow. Running away from problems is an easy thing for the subconscious mind to do. But think about what advantages you get every time you solve a problem or conflict. You build up your self-esteem and self-confidence, grow emotionally, and become a better human within.

Have the courage to encounter issues in your relationship but set a standard for conflict resolution and stick to it. Think about your partner's interest, be a respectful, caring, attentive listener, and express genuine empathy.

You should have patience when solving a relationship issue. The subconscious mind is impulsively reactive whereas a wise person is mindfully responsive to a conflict.

Life doesn't give much to those who are fearful, but it does give an abundance to those who are courageous. Add courage to all your loving attitudes:

Be courageous in your love
Be courageous in your communication
Be courageous to forgive
Be courageous to be flexible
Be courageous to respect your partner
Be courageous to take responsibility for your relationship
Be courageous to become close to your partner
Be courageous to be caring for your partner
Be courageous to solve conflicts in your relationship

When you are courageous, you act outside your comfort zone. With courage, you can overcome subconscious mind programming that is preventing you from experiencing your life in a new way. You might feel uncomfortable when you want to become close and love someone, since you may have been programmed to avoid closeness. You should have the courage to act to overcome challenges in your relationship despite being uncomfortable. The big rewards in life are given to those who act with courage and overcome their fears.

Don't Get Advice Regarding Your Relationship from Friends and Family

No matter how much your family and friends care about you, they are not experts in relationship resolutions. Your relationship should become a sacred place where you solve conflicts together without the involvement of others. Family and friends want to help you, but because they lack the skills to solve relationship conflicts, they often give wrong advice that would hurt your relationship rather than be helpful. Couples therapists, on the other hand, are trained to have the skills to resolve relationship conflicts and be unbiased. It might be a challenge not talking with your family and close friends when encountering a conflict in your relationship, especially for women who want to share and talk about how they feel about the conflict; instead, you can talk with your partner, or you can write down how you feel about the conflict on a piece of paper, so you can express your emotions. When a conflict shows up in your relationship, do your best to solve the conflict together with your partner. You can then develop the crucial problem-solving skills for a lasting, loving relationship, and your self-confidence improves. If, after your attempt to find a solution for your conflict, you couldn't find any, you can consult a couples therapist who you feel a good connection with after your first visit. You can visit a few couples therapists and choose the one with whom you feel attuned. In a conscious relationship, you are aware that conflicts are opportunities for personal and spiritual growth. Conflicts show us parts of our inner world that need to be healed. Your partner is a mirror of your inner world, and you are a mirror of your partner's inner world. Another important point to mention is that you should never share your relationship conflicts and challenges with your opposite-sex friends; doing so would be a starting point for cheating on your partner.

Don't Try to Change Your Partner

When there is a conflict in a relationship, people are inclined to focus on the problem, forget their contribution to creating the conflict, and expect their partner to change. When we expect someone to change, despite their willingness to change, we activate their inner defense system and prepare the path toward dispute and heated argument. Sometimes, they may hear what we say but forget about it a month later and continue to do what they think is right and what they are programmed in their subconscious mind to do. It is nearly impossible to change someone without their willingness; otherwise, they feel forced, creating inner resistance. You should work on your inner world and improve within yourself. When you change and enhance your energy level, you can influence your partner with your energy and attitude without saying a thing. When there is no direct verbal or nonverbal reaction to a relationship problem, your partner's inner world won't resist and won't feel forced. You can talk with your partner about changes you are making in your attitude, habits, and behavior, showing you are working on yourself to become better in your relationship, but be careful not to implicitly convey the expectation that he needs to change too. Often, your positive change motivates your partner to change as well. By doing so, you use your mental energy to improve yourself and don't waste your time and energy forcing your partner to change. The key here is not to have any expectations from your partner when you behave better and become more amicable and kinder. Perceptions, behaviors, habits, and attitudes are ingrained in the subconscious mind and create personality and character. It is true that sometimes a small change in perception or attitude or building a new habit can tremendously impact one's life; one should use the conscious mind to implement the changes required to develop a new perception, attitude, or habit. But remember, something that seems abnormal to you might seem normal to your partner. The point is that perceptions are not about who's right or wrong but about different points of view regarding a particular fact. Both of you can be right to some degree regarding a challenging fact in your relationship. However, the art of a loving relationship is to understand that your partner's perceptions are based on his programming in the subconscious mind and his belief system; regardless, treat him lovingly.

In a relationship argument, a man has evidence that proves he is right; the woman also has proof that she is right.

It is a mind trap in a relationship to try to prove who is right in a dispute. You are in a relationship, and your partner is the closest human on Earth to you; you are not in court or at university to prove something. Compromise with and understand your partner. All humans have unique perceptions and understandings of incidences and facts in life, though some have better interpretations and understandings of those incidences and facts. Of course, you can kindly share your feelings and needs with your partner, but thinking about changing your partner without their willingness is not wise. Psychology studies of humans show that nothing will help individuals unless they have a deep desire to change.

How to Turn Off the Ego's Defense Mechanism

There is a spiritual explanation about why acceptance in relationships does wonders and benefits the couple in a relationship. When you nag or criticize your partner, you activate in your partner the ego defense mechanism to protect itself. When you truly accept your partner for whoever he is, the ego defense mechanism of your partner finds nothing to fight back and is, therefore, turned off; you can then connect with your partner's true essence, which is pure love. When there is a dispute, two egos are involved in the fight because egos can't tolerate one another. When there is mutual understanding and kindness, the true being of two humans is connected.

Compromising, Neglecting, or Hiding Issues in a Relationship?

In a relationship, an issue for one person may be perceived as trivial and for another person as a dealbreaker. Sometimes you should compromise while other times you shouldn't neglect or hide an issue that emotionally bothers you. When you compromise a problem in a relationship, you are not bothered by the issue and can live with it or forget about it. Compromise is an essential skill in a loving relationship. Notwithstanding, if an issue in your relationship keeps bothering you emotionally and troubling you inside, and you neglect or hide it, you set yourself up for an unsatisfactory relationship. You may suddenly emotionally explode, and the accumulated non-expressed emotions can badly harm your relationship. Have the courage to share your feelings when something bothers you that you cannot compromise. You can use genuine communication skills (Chapter 7) and convey the message of your feelings concerning the issue to your partner in a loving way. Your mind may want to prevent you from solving the emotional outrage, but you should dare to free yourself. Your mind wants you to neglect the issue or wants you to hide it to keep the problem at bay. But choose to solve the problem and free yourself from the burden of inner emotional annoyance. Neglecting and hiding are inaction. Working on a relationship to solve problems is action. So, when there is an issue in a relationship, reflect on it to find out whether you can compromise on the issue or not; if you cannot, then begin to find a solution and solve the issue. When there is conflict in your relationship, only focus on solving that specific issue; the mind might want to go to the negative memories and fuel the fire in dispute; however, stay in the present moment and try to understand your partner's perspective. In a loving relationship, contempt has no place, and respect is the holy temple connecting your hearts. Even when there is a conflict, you should lovingly say to your partner, "What can I do to soothe you?" rather than angrily asking, "What do you want from me?" Your nonverbal communication is more important than your verbal communication. Your tone of voice, eye contact, body movement, facial expression, and inner feelings should convey the message of caring, understanding, and loving.

Life Adjustment in a New Relationship

When a new relationship begins, two people with different lifestyles come together to live under the same roof. There would be a period of lifestyle adjustment. When you begin to live with your partner, you may not sleep well for some time until you get used to the new sleeping condition. There might be differences in the kinds of food you eat and when you eat. The differences would be in other areas of life, too. You should be patient and not jump to the conclusion that your relationship doesn't feel right or things are not going well. Be flexible and accepting of your partner's lifestyle. You are moving outside your comfort zone to grow and experience a higher level of humanity and emotions.

You may say that I keep repeating the importance of patience. As a researcher of the human mind and behavior, I know that repetition is one of the few best techniques for reprogramming the subconscious mind so that a concept can be internalized and eventually expressed through mental behavior and action. Patience is the key factor in a loving relationship. Think about it often, ruminate about the different ways that patience can help your relationship, and internalize the concept of patience in your being.

Avoid the Mind Trap of Who's Right

When there is an argument in a relationship, you shouldn't try to prove who is right and who is wrong. Each side in the argument has a subconscious mind with different evidence to prove it is right and to affirm itself. Each side perceives the conflict or situation from an angle that makes sense to them. The best response to a conflict in your relationship is to try to understand your partner's point of view and perceive the situation or conflict from her perspective. A relationship is not a battlefield to prove who is right or wrong; it is a field of caring, respect, and mutual understanding. If you are arguing with your partner to prove you are right, you have lost the mind game and fallen into a mind trap. Remember that emotional reasoning is a thinking error. In an argument, it is easy to fall into the mind trap of emotional reasoning by saying, "I feel frustrated, so it is your fault;" you may not say that explicitly but implicitly. The theory of interpersonal relativity, developed by Dr. David Burns, says that one who seeks help nearly always discovers that he or she has created exactly the problem that they are complaining about. So, the right way to face a conflict is not to prove who is right or wrong; rather, you should reflect on your inner world and do some self-discovery to find out how you have contributed to the problem. Of course, the ego always resists, but you can be courageous and take responsibility. The reaction to an unwanted incident or misbehavior is usually automatic and quick, while a response is nearly always with deliberation and patience.

Keep the Stressors at Bay

Home should be your castle of peace and harmony. There are a variety of stressors in life, and if we let them come into our relationship and inside our home, they can be detrimental. Work-related stress, our partner's family and friends, financial difficulties, housework, the arrival of a new baby, health issues, and so on can have a destructive effect on our relationship if we don't neutralize or lessen their negative impacts. If you examine these stressors, you will find that they are not part of your relationship but personal stressors, and you should separate these stressors from your relationship as much as possible.

Based on biological differences between men and women, men shouldn't talk about the stressors that they have in their workplace and outside the home with their partner, as talking about stressors conveys the stress to her and imbalances the harmony in relationship and peace at home.

If you are a man and feel you need to talk about your life stressors, you should have close male friends with whom you can talk. Men's and women's relief mechanisms to stressors are different. Whereas women feel relieved when they talk about their stressors with their partner and feel emotional support and validation, men most likely prefer to be silent and not talk about their problems; they need more time alone.

In-laws and your partner's friends are part of your partner's social network; though they might cause stress in your relationship, you should be careful not to let anyone enter your *oneness* circle to negatively impact your relationship. Whatever it is, always respect your partner's family and friends and let the power of respect keep the stress imposed by family and friends at bay. Remember, love can overcome any obstacle in a relationship.

Financial difficulties can affect relationships and become a source of stress and argument. Like any other area of life, financial security is attainable through developing new constructive beliefs about money, productive habits, and learning new skills. There is no specific right or wrong way to budget your life; whatever way is accepted by both of you and is perceived as fair is the right way for you.

Housework can be a stressor, especially for women. Nowadays, most women not only work outside the home but also do housework and childcare more than men. Men should help more with housework, which has a tremendous positive impact on a relationship.

No matter what the source of stress is, don't let it affect your relationship. A stressor is a problem; you can either solve it or minimize its effect on your relationship. The point is this: keep the stressors at bay to maintain your peace and protect your loving relationship.

Flexibility in Relationships Is Empowering

When two people begin a relationship, they bring many different traits and behaviors into the relationship. People from the same culture and even the same family or neighborhood can be substantially different from one another. When entering a relationship with someone you love, it means you have an opportunity to grow in love. However, there might be areas of life in which you are not in harmony with each other. Flexibility in a relationship can be a gift to both parties. When you are flexible, you stimulate your brain to regenerate new cells, and the brain's plasticity is activated to keep your brain young rather than being rigid and inflexible. It also sends a message of love to your partner that you care for her. Be accepting toward change and growth.

So, being flexible in a relationship is a wise response. In a lasting, loving relationship, compromise is a powerful tool for staying together. Why compromise? Because you love, and, as Rumi says, "Love doesn't have any reason; only love explains love."

If you want to experience something different in your relationship, you should change your perception of love and improve your habitual way of thinking and behavior. The relationship that you are in is the fruit of your thoughts and behavior. If you want to experience a different quality in your relationship, you should think and behave differently.

Better Know Men: An Insight for Women

The male mind is a problem solver and is analytical; that's why when his woman shares her feelings, he tries to analyze the situation, find a solution, and solve her problem rather than attentively listening to his woman, validating her feelings, and attuning with his woman's state of mind. In other ways, a man expects his woman to appreciate what he does in the relationship, trust him, and accept him for who he is. Finding flaws in your man and repeatedly pointing them out damages his self-confidence and activates his inner world defense system, causing heated arguments or withdrawal. Men are goal-oriented; if they don't have a specific goal, they are lost in life. Men want to be independent and detached. Freedom and time alone are important to them. They usually commit to a relationship when they genuinely want to establish a lasting relationship with someone they love. Men often think about competition rather than cooperation and are more assertive and direct than women in their expressions, and they can be tough. Testosterone is a hormone associated with strength, bone mass, fat distribution, and muscle size. A man's testosterone is ten to thirty times more than a woman's.

Don't try to change or correct your man but, rather, appreciate his good qualities. When a woman tries to correct or change her man, she implicitly sends the message that "you are not good enough; you are defective; I don't accept you as you are." When a man feels that he is not accepted, he feels humiliated, and his self-confidence is weakened. He either explicitly enters a dispute with his woman or withdraws and makes emotional and physical distance. Trusting a man means affirming and acknowledging honestly that he is doing his best in life and the relationship and that he is good and adequate as he is. When you trust your man and express genuine acceptance, you boost your man's self-confidence and testosterone. Consequently, he wants to do something good in return for feeling great. One of a man's greatest joys and pleasures is to make his woman happy. In challenging situations and stressed moments, men tend to be left alone and not talk about their feelings; they need some space to contemplate internally about the problem. Men are prone to avoid talking about sensitive issues, and that perhaps is because they are less skillful than women in handling stressful incidents and topics. To avoid becoming overwhelmed with stressful topics and marital conflicts, men may look down, avoid eye contact, or become silent.

Better Know Women: An Insight for Men

Women are relationship-oriented, and their world is full of emotion. Family and friends are extremely important for women, but that doesn't mean their beloved partner is less important. However, you should always respect a woman's family and friends and never criticize them. Women are intuitive, which may be the reason why they expect you to intuitively know their feelings and be responsive to their emotional needs without communicating with you. However, you can use genuine communication techniques to clearly understand your woman's feelings and be responsive to her emotional needs. Women feel vulnerable when they want to open their heart, but they should trust you first. They represent the beauty and delicacy of the creation; they are virtuous. Always treat your woman with tenderness and delicacy. Women are the world of love. If you enter the heart of a woman, you win her soul. In their true nature, women are nurturing, cooperative, and responsive. Throughout history, women have been nurturing and providing for kids and families; nurturing is part of women's DNA, and that would explain why women like shopping, and you should be patient when your partner is shopping. Women have an unlimited capacity for love; they are interdependent and need to connect with other people in their network. The more good girlfriends a woman has, the happier she is and the better her relationship with her man will be. So, understand that the close relationship of your woman with her girlfriends benefits you.

A woman wants you to be affectionate and compliment her at every opportunity. She wants your attention and meaningful conversation. She wants your emotional support when she is emotionally stressed and overwhelmed. She wants your tenderness even when things get tough. She wants your care and understanding. She wants you to treat her with respect and kindness, no matter what happens. She wants to be cherished. Women think about "what feels right." Women want to share their feelings and "feel felt." A woman wants your empathy in her struggles, challenges, and triumphs.

Estrogen is a female hormone and is related to the development of reproductive and sexual organs in women. A woman's body usually has ten to thirty times more estrogen than men's.

Helping with household chores means a lot to a woman. Women have many responsibilities these days imposed on them by social structure. They should work outside of the home and have income; they should take care of their home, children, and their man; they should prepare food for the family and also take care of themselves and look beautiful; these are a lot of works, and many women are stressed. When you, as a man, do some household chores, it reduces the burden on your woman's shoulder, decreases her stress, and means a lot to her.

A comprehensive study at the University of Tennessee suggests that a woman's anger usually falls into one to three categories: powerlessness, unfairness, and irresponsibility. Be *one* with your woman; share power, be fair with her, and avoid behavior conveying the message of irresponsibility.

Honor your words and don't show off who you are not; simply be yourself and let your honesty build your relationship. Women need to feel emotionally and physically safe to open up for closeness. Don't overlook the power of trustworthiness and sincerity in creating a meaningful, long-term relationship.

Ask your woman about her worries and perspective of the future, what makes her happy in life, and how you could have more romance and enjoyment together. Show genuine care and interest in her life. Women are not made for argument or criticism but for love and respect. Women need to talk in tough situations and stressful moments to feel relieved. Practice always being a good listener to your woman with attentiveness and empathy. Always validate your woman's feelings and emotions, give her a hug when she is emotional, and try to do something for her to reduce her stress. Ask your woman to talk with you; hear her inner world every day. Ask about her life, worries, challenges, victories, etc. The more she talks to you, the more she feels feminine and connected to her core being. Talking stimulates the production of estrogen in women and reduces their stress levels. Women are generally better than men in bringing up sensitive issues and talking about problems, and they are more skillful than men in coping with stress. Incorporate attention, affection, humor, caring, and support into connection with your woman.

Write down below the key points you learned in Chapter 6.

Chapter 7

Genuine Communication: A Key Element in a Thriving Relationship

Genuine Communication

There is a myth about romance that if someone loves you, he must intuitively know how you feel and what you want. This unrealistic expectation often leads to frustration and turmoil. The problem is that sometimes we don't even know what we want but expect that our partner knows what we want. Genuine communication helps us clearly communicate, share our emotions, and express our wants and needs.

Words Are Powerful; Use Them Wisely

What do you talk about with your partner? Are your talks uplifting, neutral, or disheartening? When you talk about any topic, you activate neural circuits in the brain that produce hormones accordingly. Why not talk about your dreams together? Why not talk about your wonderful experiences in the past, like your honeymoon? Your beautiful memories of the past are a precious asset you should use to bring more joy to your relationship. Train your mind to talk about your beautiful moments from the past and the best possible scenarios for the future. Dream together and enjoy the good feeling of being together. A Persian proverb says, "Description of pleasure has half its joy." By just talking and describing pleasurable moments, you are enjoying half of their joy without experiencing them in reality. So, in your conversation, make it a habit to talk about your beautiful past moments, your enjoyable current experiences, and your dreams.

Six Steps for Genuine Communication

Some studies suggest that the primary challenge that most couples encounter in their relationships is miscommunication or misunderstanding. Whatever your mind is telling you about your communication capabilities, there is always room for improvement. Assign some time during the week to practice genuine communication skills by doing the following six steps.

1. Listen Attentively without Distractions

When you listen attentively to your partner, your behavior implies that your partner is important to you and that you care for her.

2. Don't Interrupt Your Partner

Let your partner talk as much as she wants to talk. Keep eye contact and use your posture and gestures to imply that you are carefully listening to her. You can encourage your partner to talk more by saying, "Tell me more," or "What else?"

3. Don't Judge Your Partner

When listening to your partner, don't judge her verbally or even in your mind.

4. Restate What Your Partner Said to Validate Your Understanding

After your partner has expressed what she wanted to say, restate what she has just said and ask whether you have understood her correctly.

5. Ask Your Partner How She Feels

You don't want to second guess your partner's feelings. Simply ask her how she feels and validate her feelings.

6. Find a Piece of Truth in Your Partner's Words

Often, when your partner criticizes you, there is some degree of truth in what she says. Be humble, and don't feel defensive. Find a piece of truth (as little as a mustard seed!) in what your partner tells you and acknowledge her expression.

Genuine communication skills are a vital factor in a loving relationship. You should educate yourself about these skills and apply them in your relationship. Continuous practice yields excellence. In the beginning, you may not be good at applying genuine communication; however, read the six steps I mentioned above a few times every day and practice the knowledge you have learned to understand your partner better and respond to her needs.

Men should be careful when they listen to their women. Do not try to downplay the problem or the situation your partner is talking about by saying, "That's not a big deal," "Don't worry; it will be fine," or something like that. Do not give solutions to your partner unless she asks for your advice. Make sure to show genuine care and empathy and validate her feelings. After your partner expresses herself completely, hug her for about five seconds with emotion.

Be Specific When Discussing an Issue

When discussing a relationship issue or other problems, be very specific and avoid vague language. For instance, instead of saying to your partner, "You don't care about me," say something like, "Last Sunday, when you went with your sister to the shopping mall without me, I felt inferior and taken for granted."

When you use the pronoun "You" to discuss an issue in a relationship and use vague language, it is usually blaming your partner, and that activates the defense mechanism in your partner's subconscious mind to react; so, communication may not lead to the desired output and even end in a heated argument. When you discuss a conflict with your partner, you should be as specific as possible by addressing the four elements related to the conflict: when, where, what, and who. And share your feelings by saying, "I felt, or I feel…." Don't assume that your partner should know how you interpret situations. Genuine communication helps you express to your partner what an event or behavior means to you to avoid miscommunication, using vague language, or burying your feelings.

Special Note for Men

Men especially should pay attention to this topic. Women are full of emotions. You should pay careful attention when your life partner talks to you. This is how a woman can express her emotions and feel relieved. Most of the time, when your partner talks with you about her problems, she is not looking for a solution; *she wants your empathy, validation, understanding, and undivided attention.*

Empathy is different from sympathy. Empathy is seeing the situation through your partner's eyes and genuinely acknowledging that how she feels makes sense. Sympathy, on the other hand, is to perceive the problem from your side and have a sense of pity for your partner. Show genuine interest in hearing your woman through verbal and non-verbal communication to help her talk and share more about her feelings. Often say to her, "Tell me more about it" or "What else? I want to understand it better" to encourage your woman to talk more with you. By doing so, you make your woman feel good.

Anxious Attachment Style and Genuine Communication

People with an anxious attachment style usually emotionally depend on their partner or whom they are emotionally attached to. They don't express their emotions that they think would make their partner run away or feel offended.

Here is a story to clarify the communication style in anxious-avoidant dating. Lisa is dating Theodore and feels very attracted to him. After several months, while everything is apparently going well, Theodore has not introduced Lisa to his family and friends. Lisa also feels that Theodore doesn't like much physical contact. It has happened a few times that after having quality time together, Theodore disappeared for a few days and did not contact Lisa. All of these events and behavior show that Lisa has entered a difficult relationship with a man with an avoidant attachment style. For Theodore, any closeness is unconsciously perceived as a threat, and his subconscious mind does everything possible to prevent closeness. It looks like Theodore prefers to keep their relationship secret and foggy. Though Lisa feels frustrated at times about Theodore's behavior, she does not talk about how she feels to avoid potential conflict that might lead to losing Theodore forever. The challenge is that, usually, people don't know their attachment style, and they don't know why they behave in a certain way.

Lisa should stand for herself and respect her feelings. Lisa should *convince* herself that she deserves love and affection. She should clearly communicate with Theodore that she feels inferior and unimportant when he keeps things secret and doesn't introduce her to his family and friends. She could say something like this to Theodore at an appropriate time: "When we had a good time together on Tuesday, I was expecting your call the next day, but I didn't hear from you until Sunday. I feel our relationship doesn't seem serious to you."

Through genuine communication with Theodore at the beginning of the relationship, Lisa could avoid a painful relationship in the future. And if she feels Theodore doesn't care for her feelings, she should end the relationship before opening her heart to a loving relationship. *Caring is at the heart of loving someone.* Theodore doesn't care about how Lisa feels, so he doesn't have the ability to love her because he is unfamiliar with the feeling of love. Lisa doesn't blame Theodore for who he is; however, she should feel that her feelings are worthy of his respect. Theodore might want to know more about the cause of his behavior and gradually learn to be emotionally open and closer to Lisa. When someone is humble enough to accept his flaws, there is big hope for improvement and growth.

One challenge for people with anxious attachment style is that they feel the person they are in love with is the only human who can make their relationship wonderful and their life happy. The truth is that no matter how wonderful and unique they perceive their partner or the one to whom they are emotionally attached, billions of humans live on Earth; many of them are amazing, and they can choose one with whom they can build a loving relationship. Developing genuine communication skills is pivotal in learning the art of a loving relationship.

A powerful mental attitude one can develop is finding and saying something good and uplifting when the conversation gets tough. Genuine communication has a focal ingredient: respect. Whatever the situation, always remind yourself that you are talking and listening to the closest human to you.

Avoid Passive Aggression in Your Emotional Expressions

Passive aggression is when a partner in a relationship indirectly and silently expresses his inner emotional conflicts, frustration, pain, or anger.

Edward is the master of passive aggression. He is frustrated about kitchen messiness and unwashed dishes all over. Lily is not used to organizing and cleaning after meals; instead, she prefers to wait for the following day to clean the kitchen. Edward is upset about her behavior. Despite talking to Lily a few times about the issue that deeply bothers him, Lily continues her old habit of cleaning the kitchen and unwashed dishes the next day. Edward stops talking to Lily and decreases his communication to the minimum. He is angry inside, but his face shows no sign of rage. He intentionally makes mistakes when grocery shopping to take revenge on Lily's neglect of kitchen cleanliness. He also procrastinates about fixing their home roof, which has been damaged and needs repair. In his mind, he is not violent and abusive; he does not scream at Lily or beat her. However, he is not aware that what he is doing is passive aggression; it is as bad as assertive aggression; the difference is that it happens in silence and ruins his relationship with Lily. While a woman's natural need is to talk, he doesn't talk with Lily; Lily feels bad, and her emotions are overwhelming. She talks with Edward, but he refuses to engage in any conversation. Edward is silently violent.

Many of us might have been engaged in passive-aggressive behavior here and there and thought that it was okay. No! It is not okay to be passive-aggressive and injure others' feelings. Passive aggression demonstrates *indifference,* which is the opposite of love. If you love someone, you care for their feelings.

Think about how you treat your partner in your current or past relationships and see whether you have engaged in passive-aggressive behavior. Reflection on one's behavior can be eye-opening and help prevent further damage to the relationship. If there is some issue in your relationship that continuously bothers you internally, and you don't effectively communicate with your partner to solve the problem, you might unknowingly engage in passive aggression. Even if you are continuously upset at your partner for her behavior, and you don't talk about it in a loving manner, you are in the process of passive aggression.

Technology and Relationships in the Modern Age

The world has dramatically changed in the last decades. Technology has made life a lot easier. Communications have become extremely faster than before. However, the side effects of technology on human life have not been studied as fast as technological advancement. Using technology, particularly the Internet, is obviously stealing our attention. We talked about how caring is at the core of your expression of love in a loving relationship. But how can you be caring for your partner if you spend hours on social media, TV, games, or other modern entertainment? Is it caring if, while your partner is talking with you, you look at your cell phone or are distracted by any other electronic devices? Humans have become closer in the virtual world where no natural emotional interactions exist, and yet they feel lonelier than ever.

Build a constructive habit of using technology that enhances the quality of your relationship. You can set a rule that, for example, after nine o'clock at night, both of you should not use your cell phone, turn the notification sounds and ring off, or set the cell phone on airplane mode. Your relationship needs your care and attention, but technology is competing for both.

Imagine a family sitting together as everyone is busy with their cell phone, and communications between them are minimal or distracted. The family is paying a high cost for neglecting the most crucial factor of a happy life: quality relationships. An eighty-five-year Harvard study has shown that quality relationships are the major contributors to a happy life, health, and longevity.

We should manage our technology usage and not let technology drive our lives. We have created technology, and we shouldn't let it consume us. Make a plan to spend quality time with your partner without any distractions from technology. Show that you care much more for your partner than for technology.

Write down below the key points you learned in Chapter 7.

Chapter 8

Constructive Habits and Personality Attributes in a Loving Relationship

Integrity

Integrity creates a charming and influential character. When what you think and feel are in harmony with what you say and do, you have integrity. What comes from your heart touches your beloved's soul.

In neuroscience, integration is a process that creates a *coherent self* through the flow of energy and information across times and contexts. Integration creates a sense of *self* on the subjective dimension. The smoother that the flow of energy and information passes through all layers of memory in the past and present moment and the certainty about the future, the more serenity the individual experiences. When you have integrity, you are at peace and harmony with yourself.

Integrity in a relationship endows clarity and eludes sending mixed messages to your partner, thus preventing confusion, misunderstanding, and misperception. When you notice something beautiful about your partner, express your appreciation and admiration to your partner with integrity. You may say, "What if I see something in my partner that I don't like?" I say, "You can still express how you feel to your partner, but you should always express yourself in a loving, respectful manner." Your expression should be soft, maintaining your integrity by staying serene and authentic. If you express yourself harshly, chances are very high that you activate the defense mechanism in your partner, and you end up in a heated, long argument. However, when you start expressing yourself softly and gently, conveying vulnerability and kindness through your tone of voice, facial expression, and body language, you may activate empathy in your partner and see a much better result than expected.

Integrity emanates trust and commitment in a relationship. You accept your partner because he has integrity. With your integrity, your partner can trust and accept you; trusting and accepting your partner is the foundation for a meaningful, long-term relationship.

Respect in Relationship

Respect is a non-negotiable human right. Regardless of what a person has said or done, they deserve to be respected. Despite the universal right of respect for humans, we might not comply with this human right as we become frustrated, angry, or stressed. Humans want respect, as they feel worthy and wanted when they are respected.

In a relationship, you should always treat your partner with respect and courtesy. Isn't your partner the closest human to you? Isn't your partner your beloved? Doesn't it make sense to treat the closest human to you with the highest level of respect?

When we are triggered by a situation or behavior in a relationship, we may not respond to the situation with courtesy and react impulsively. The reaction is an automatic program in the subconscious mind, quick and usually without conscious mind interference. Your mind's programming has been created by your parents (primary caregivers), family, media, friends, and environment. When something happens that is not aligned with what you expect, you become frustrated and say a bad word that you have heard thousands of times in movies and with friends. The bad word has been ingrained in your subconscious mind and has become the automatic reaction to an unwanted situation or behavior. But this automatic behavior is destructive in your relationship and eludes closeness and lovingness. The first step is to observe your behavior and detect your reaction when you feel frustrated, angry, or stressed. If you realize your reaction toward your partner is disrespectful, you should find a respectful response to alter the defensive one. Remember that you don't want to blame yourself or others for your destructive reaction. Use your mental energy to develop a positive response when frustrated, angry, or stressed. Write down your response on a piece of paper or any other way that reminds you of your constructive response. Changing your destructive reaction to a constructive response may take a few weeks to a few months. It takes time and effort to develop courteous behavior, but the reward of treating your partner with love and respect is enormous. Make a rule in your relationship and commit to following it to always treat your partner respectfully. In the beginning, you may sometimes fail to comply with this rule, but if it happens, accept it and tell yourself, "Even though I couldn't treat my partner with courtesy this time, I am determined and committed to love and respect her (him) always."

How to Maintain Respect between You

Respect is an essential element in a loving relationship. How can love be without respect? When you love someone, you respect her. When you feel deep admiration for your beloved's character, personality, abilities, and achievements, you genuinely respect your partner. When you express your admiration through verbal and nonverbal communication, you indirectly tell your partner that you respect her. But how can one maintain respect in a relationship? *Honor your word, be yourself, and strive to become a better version of yourself.* Excessive fantasizing about your partner's personality, character, qualities, and achievements can set you up for disappointment and cause you to lose respect for your partner when you know he does not meet your expectations or cannot fulfill your fantasized predictions.

For instance, a woman assumes her partner is very rich and marries him, and then she finds out that her husband is considerably in debt; she might lose respect for her husband. If one side in a relationship hides too many flaws and pretends to have many good qualities, she will lose respect when they begin to live together, and the truth starts to show up. That is why being yourself at the very beginning of dating others is important; it conveys the message of honesty and sincerity, which are actually attractive and bring a lot of respect. If someone wants you for whoever you are, you will have a much better relationship in the long run. In a long-term relationship, sometimes a partner advances later in his career or education, which might cause him to lose respect for his partner and incite his feeling of superiority. In a loving relationship, respect is unconditional; no matter what happens, a couple respects each other because they love each other and because love does not need a reason; love is the reason.

The Only Source to Receive Feminine and Masculine Energy

I have seen old couples still passionate about each other after more than fifty years in their relationships. The man, like a moth revolving around a candle, revolves around his beloved. A human being is a mixture of feminine and masculine energies. The feminine energy dominates in women, and the masculine energy dominates in men. Men need more soothing feminine energy, and women need more powerful masculine energy. Men and women are attracted to each other to exchange energy. When you are in a relationship, and the only source of masculine or feminine energy you are looking for is your partner, you passionately want your partner.

If you are a man, you want to get your feminine energy only from the woman you are in a relationship with, not from your female colleagues, your just-friend girlfriends, or any other women. You don't waste your masculine energy on others and keep so little for your partner. You keep all your masculine energy for your partner and receive the feminine energy only from her. Any flirting with other women is an exchange of masculine and feminine energy outside your relationship, and it hurts your relationship; watching porn products eats up masculine energy and is detrimental to a relationship.

The same is true for women. If you are exchanging feminine and masculine energies with your male colleagues, just-friend boyfriends, or any other men in your life, your feminine energy is wasted outside your relationship, and it harms your relationship.

In a relationship, the best scenario for friendships is that the man has a circle of close boyfriends, and the woman has a circle of close girlfriends. When a man spends time with his boyfriends, he amplifies his masculine energy; when a woman spends time with her girlfriends, she boosts her feminine energy. As they come together with their increased masculine and feminine energies, they are attracted to each other like magnets.

In order to keep a relationship passionate, both men and women should protect their masculine and feminine energies outside of their relationship, enhancing their femininity and masculinity by having circles of friendships of only girlfriends for the women and only boyfriends for the men.

Institute the Concept of *Oneness* in Your Relationship

When you want to mature in love and build a loving relationship, you should practice internalizing the concept of *oneness* with your partner. Some people may use the word *weness* for a relationship, but whatever word you want to use, *oneness* or *weness* should be a fundamental element in your relationship. You are not alone anymore. You have begun a relationship with another human being with hopes, needs, aspirations, flaws, and goodness. Your partner's interests should feel like your interests. The concept of *oneness* becomes even more important when a couple have their first baby. The arrival of the newborn baby is fantastic but can be a challenge for the relationship. I have seen couples divorce soon after having their first child. Why does this happen? Because when the newborn comes, the mother goes under tremendous hormonal changes and produces a lot of oxytocin for her newborn baby. Oxytocin causes a maternal feeling when she touches, gazes, and breastfeeds her newborn. A mother's love for her newborn baby is a physiological and emotional process and is necessary for the survival of the human species. But the man feels separated from the concept of *oneness*. Though he is the father of the newborn baby, he somehow feels left alone. The focus of the mother becomes her newborn baby. The solution is to protect the concept of *oneness* in any situation, including the arrival of a newborn baby. A man should actively support his wife emotionally and help her in any way that decreases her burden of being a mother and her stress; now, three persons are involved in the concept of *oneness*.

When you institute the concept of *oneness* in your relationship, you are always together and support each other emotionally or with whatever means possible. The relationship with a partner is much deeper than that with a close friend. The goal of a loving relationship is to become *one*, and the *oneness* between you and your partner should not be disturbed by anything or anyone.

Caring Is the Heart of Loving

If you love someone, you care about her. It doesn't matter how busy you are; you figure out how to find some time to care about your beloved. The subject is no longer *I* but *You*.

What do you want?
What do you like?
What can I do for you today to make you happy?

The ego thinks about the *self*, while in love, the lover thinks about the beloved. In love, caring about the *self* evolves into caring about the *beloved*. The beloved's happiness is the lover's purpose. Caring implicitly conveys the message that the beloved is important and deserves your attention. Caring requires empathy, and empathy asks for understanding. There is a saying, "To love you is to know you," which makes sense, as to care for someone, you should know her. What does your beloved like? What doesn't your beloved like? What challenges is your beloved facing in life? How can you help your beloved overcome challenges? What are your beloved's dreams? What can you do to make your beloved feel secure and loved? What are your beloved's fears and hopes? What does your beloved's ideal life look like? And asking many more questions to understand your beloved is a lifelong journey to mature and evolve in love. Life is not a destination but a journey toward *higher self* and spiritual growth, and caring is at the core of loving. When you commit to your beloved, you care for your beloved's feelings and your relationship; when you respect your beloved, you care for your beloved's emotions and dignity; when you make your beloved happy, you care for your beloved's happiness; when you accept your beloved, you care for your beloved's being with all flaws and goodness; when you demonstrate empathy with your beloved, you care for your beloved's emotional well-being. And in one word, you deeply care for your beloved because you love your partner. The antonym of love is not hatred, or dislike; it is *indifference*. If you don't care, it means you don't love. Understanding why caring is at the heart of loving is not difficult.

Value Each Other: An Ongoing Attitude in a Loving Relationship

Do you know what the root causes of being bored are in life? Taking our blessings for granted and not seeing and valuing what we already have. When we take good things in life for granted, we stop enjoying them. It feels like they don't exist for us anymore. If you want to enjoy your relationship and build a lasting, loving relationship, you should never take your partner for granted. Life gets busy and fast; to live life to the fullest, we should reduce the speed of life, contemplate what we have, and activate the mental attitude of gratitude. Taking your partner for granted implicitly conveys the message that you are *indifferent* about your partner's presence and that she is no longer important. How can you prevent taking your partner for granted? Develop a mental attitude of thankfulness for your partner's presence in your life and enjoy your partner's presence. If you don't enjoy your partner anymore, it means you have taken her for granted. Taking the blessings we have for granted is ungratefulness.

In a loving relationship, your beloved's presence in your life is the source of tranquility, enjoyment, love, compassion, and kindness. See the beauties in your partner every day, acknowledge them, enjoy them, compliment them, feel good about them, and be grateful for being in your relationship. When the mind is busy, we don't see marvelous things surrounding us; we live in a busy mind, not in touch with life. We should practice living in the present moment, not letting our mind transport us to the unknown future and inaccessible past. Set some time every day to enjoy your beloved and feel gratitude for her presence. Feeling gratitude for the presence of your beloved and her contribution to your life should be one of the fundamental habits you develop for building a loving relationship. Initially, it asks for your mental energy and effort, but you should be aware of the danger of taking your partner for granted, which can ruin your relationship. The mind's tendency to take blessings for granted must be harnessed. You want to direct your attention to the good things you have in life. One key skill for a loving relationship is living in the present moment, appreciating and enjoying your partner every day, and not letting your mind take your beloved for granted. If you take your partner for granted, it means that your subconscious mind is ruling your relationship, and your relationship is on autopilot. But when you begin to pay attention to your partner and feel and express gratitude, you are in a real relationship. Develop an attitude of appreciation and gratitude toward your beloved and your relationship. Perceive everything your beloved does, including housework, cooking, shopping, and so on, *as a favor, not a duty,* and genuinely thank your partner continuously. When you thank your partner for what he shares and does in your relationship, you implicitly say to your partner that you have noticed his contribution to your relationship, and you are grateful toward him. Studies show that in happy relationships, couples notice almost every little thing their partner does that contributes to their relationship, whereas, in unhappy relationships, couples overlook, ignore, or discount what their partner contributes to their relationship in everyday life.

Develop a Habit of Appreciation and Compliment

A habit is a settled way of thinking and behavior that usually repeatedly occurs and needs minimum mental energy. One of the precious mental attitudes is the habit of genuine appreciation and compliments. Humans typically feel good when they see their contribution to the relationship, good traits, and physical or personal characteristics seen, appreciated, and complimented. In a relationship, appreciation and compliments shouldn't be an occasional incident but a daily ritual and habit. The vital part of appreciating and complimenting your partner is being genuine and honest in your words. How can one make a habit of appreciation and compliment? In the beginning, making a habit takes work because your conditioned mind resists changes. Your mind doesn't want to go under extra work to create new neural pathways and circuits in your brain for a new habit. However, your mind must follow your decision. You decide to build a new habit, and with patience, determination, and persistence, you can build a new constructive habit that yields enormous advantages for the rest of your life without much effort after its institution.

The more you repeat a new behavior, the easier that behavior becomes and the closer you are to building a lasting habit. No matter what you have learned in the past and how you have been programmed to treat your partner, you can change and advance in life and relationships. I can't emphasize enough how much *daily* appreciation and compliments of your partner are essential for the prosperity and quality of your relationship. Your compliment can be your genuine verbal expression of a good trait of your partner or appreciation of something your partner is doing in life or has done in the past. You could talk to your partner to know what makes her feel most appreciated or how you can compliment her so that she feels good. Think and be creative about how you can appreciate and compliment your partner.

If you want to consider the gender psychology aspect of appreciation and compliment and get the most out of this constructive habit, women should focus on appreciating their man for what he does or has done, and men should focus on complimenting their woman for her beautiful traits, physical characteristics, and personality attributes.

Be careful not to fall into the ego trap of feeling superior when your partner compliments and appreciates you daily. Feeling superior in a relationship causes emotional distance and impedes a loving relationship.

Nourish Your Relationship

In one of Rumi's poetry collections, there is a story about an infatuated lover who persists in seeing his beloved. He keeps sending messages to his beloved, "I want to see you; please come!" One night, the beloved comes to see him after midnight, but the lover is sleeping. The beloved puts a few walnuts in her lover's pocket and leaves a note for him, "Better you play with the walnuts; you are not ready for love yet."

This simple story tells that the path of love is not easy. Like learning other skills, one should invest energy and time to become skillful in the art of loving. The problem usually arises when we wait and expect others to change. We forget or neglect what we can contribute to the relationship to nourish our connection with our partner. The easy way to conduct an argument is to blame the other person when there is a conflict. When you blame others for something, you free yourself of any responsibility and possible contribution to the issue. Knowing that blaming comes from the ego is eye-opening. The ego doesn't want to change, seeing itself as perfect and viewing others as problem-makers. The more we carry this perspective of self-idealization and belittling and blaming others, the closer we are to the ego's perception. The antidote to the ego is to be humble when a conflict arises and do self-reflection to see your possible contribution to the problem.

In a relationship, we should learn how to become a better human being. One should often think, "How can I contribute to the relationship?" Why? Because of love. And if it bothers you to be a giver without expectations in a relationship, your relationship is not based on love but on self-interest. I don't want you to feel bad; however, acceptance of truth is a crucial part of human growth and maturity. You can accept what it is in your relationship and move toward what you want it to be.

When you neglect to care for your garden, weeds grow everywhere, but when you care about your garden, you assign time and energy to gardening. You nourish your garden, and thus you'll have a beautiful garden. And you do so continuously. You don't pay attention to the garden once a year. You take care of your garden at weekly intervals to ensure there are no weeds or pests in your garden. A relationship also needs to be nourished. It asks for your attention and continuous planning to grow in love and humanity.

You should assign some time every week to evaluate your behavior in your relationship and see how you can become a better lover. Of course, you should appreciate yourself as well. Self-appreciation should not induce the feeling of superiority in the relationship with your partner.

How to Keep Passion Alive in Long-Term Relationships

Women are physiologically and psychologically different from men. Women and men should indeed have equal rights, but equality does not mean sameness. Certain works are associated with femininity and produce feminine hormones. When women are involved in those activities, they recognize more of their true nature and of who they really are. The working environments are masculine in characteristics that require decision-making, leadership, competition, dealing with stressful coworkers, and so on, all of which demand a high amount of testosterone production in women's bodies. Testosterone is a male hormone, and excessive testosterone production in the female body causes more stress in her body and psyche, an increase in cortisol, and a decrease in estrogen, the feminine hormone. In response to the masculine working environments and social norms, women have developed a secondary characteristic that is closer to masculinity and further from their true nature of femininity.

And the situation for men has changed as well. Nowadays, men are involved in more routine tasks such as housekeeping, babysitting, and cooking. These routines don't require men's bodies to produce adequate testosterone, which is the masculine hormone for competition and hardship. So, on many occasions, we see couples in which the man has low testosterone and high estrogen while the woman has excessive testosterone and low estrogen. The result of such an imbalance in hormones is a cold relationship in which couples live together more like teammates than passionate lovers.

Women should deliberately engage in some feminine activities that they love the most and are possible for them to do, given their life situation. Women come back home after long hours of work and want to do some masculine behavior at home: being silent and left alone. A feminine activity helps women produce more estrogen, decrease cortisol, and relax for some time; women talking with their man about how their day was going, challenges, stressors, and good things that happened during the day is also soothing. Talking and expressing emotions are feminine activities, while being silent and aloof are masculine behaviors that won't help women experience a loving relationship. You don't need to have masculinity when you are with your man. You want to feel more feminine and connect with your deepest true nature.

On the other hand, men need some time after their stressful work to be left alone and silent to restore their testosterone level and feel good. If you are a woman, let your man have some solitude time after work and be quiet; be patient and give him enough time to restore his testosterone level.

If you want more passion in your life, you should deliberately divide chores aligned with each other's nature. For example, men should take care of emergencies such as fixing a broken roof or car. Men should actively be involved in decision-making and planning while respecting the opinions of their women. They should lead the family with tenderness and care. Taking risks and working hard are also masculine activities.

At home, women should engage more with routine tasks such as cooking and housekeeping. They should feel loved and desired by their man. The following are some activities that help women produce more estrogen and feel more feminine: Talking, hugging, dating, kissing, receiving compliments, feeling loved, being reassured, having a lot less to-do lists, getting a haircut, getting a pedicure or massage, praying, receiving help and support, and many more.

And what is the result when men have a lot more testosterone and lower estrogen than their woman and when women have a lot more estrogen and lower testosterone than their man? An ongoing passion in their relationships. If you are interested in knowing more about how to bring passion back to your relationship, I highly recommend John Gary's book *Beyond Mars and Venus,* in which he extensively explains what a man and woman need to do in the modern age to keep passion alive in their relationship.

Enjoying Life Together

Everyone wants to enjoy life and is striving to make life more pleasurable. We begin a relationship to feel better and happier and experience a higher level of emotional well-being. So, in a relationship, it is important to keep the enjoyment of life alive and flourishing. You don't do much at the beginning of a relationship and during your honeymoon, yet you feel good and happy. Usually, everything about your partner and activities together seem interesting and exciting. Novelties in getting to know your partner and his lifestyle and new experiences that you have together spike the dopamine hormone in your brain and make you feel good and content. But when the honeymoon is over and life begins its routine, the novelties gradually diminish, as does the dopamine hormone. In a conscious relationship, you should be aware that the enjoyment of life with your partner should be a priority in your life. You should allocate some time and plan your life so that you can enjoy life together, rather than letting your life routine control your pleasurable activities. You should use your creativity and find new ways to enjoy your life together. For example, you can go to a new coffee shop and try their drink and food together. Sometimes, you may not be satisfied with the new foods or store service, but you may discover a new place or meal you love; you wouldn't know if you didn't try. You can also discover various cuisines from other countries together and enjoy a new meal every time. You can visit other counties, villages, and towns close to where you live and discover their architecture, stores, and natural beauties. Traveling together is a great way to boost your dopamine hormone and feel satisfied and content in your relationship.

Don't let limiting beliefs stop you from introducing new experiences into your life. For example, don't say, "I don't have time to try new things." When you truly give priority to enjoying life with your partner, you will find time to do something together that works well, given your life situation. But enjoying life with your partner needs your attention; it requires your creativity and planning. Many novelties may occur when you enter a trip without planning; you just begin a journey and see where it goes. Ambiguity might seem fearful, but novelties and spikes of the feeling-good dopamine hormone are the prizes for facing ambiguities and experiencing unknowns. Enjoyment of life with your partner should be an everlasting part of your relationship. Seek to explore the world around you, fulfill your desires, and anticipate excitement and enjoyment with your partner. Life will never be the same, as countless extraordinary experiences exist to explore.

Act as Emotionally Intelligent Couples

Self-discovery is the foundation for developing emotional intelligence. When we know ourselves better, we know our triggers and reactions and observe our behavior, responding appropriately to triggers. We become better self-regulators of our emotions and feelings and assert our needs with respect and gentleness. Through eye contact and attentive listening without distractions, you can become more empathetic by mindful attention to your partner when she talks to you. You are aware of the motives in your relationship, such as the desire for closeness and romance, the desire to love and to be loved, and the desire to give and receive emotional support. You don't try to change your partner and let her be who she is, yet you provide support for your partner to grow and flourish in life and in your relationship. Emotionally intelligent couples are perceptive, allowing them to look at things from their partner's point of view.

Knowing each other should become a perpetual discovery in your relationship. If your partner's emotional well-being is important to you as a lover, how can you contribute to your partner's life if you are unaware of her inner world? When you get to know your partner better, you can better respond to her needs and desires. When you know your partner's likes, dislikes, worries, hopes, dreams, goals, challenges, and stressors, you can support and express your empathy and understanding to your partner. Ask your partner how you can support her and reduce her pressure in life; at times, we may not know how to help our partner, and what we think is helpful may not make much of a difference.

Studies suggest that emotional intelligence is a skill that is learnable. Whatever your attachment style is, you can develop emotional intelligence characteristics, fostering a more loving relationship with your partner. It requires your willingness to change and enter an unfamiliar path that might make you uncomfortable. Act as if you are an emotionally intelligent partner and embrace the initial discomfort to open the door to a higher level of connection, emotional exhilaration, and a loving relationship.

Be available to your partner as much as possible when she needs you. For instance, you are watching your favorite hockey team competition; your spouse wants to talk to you; you turn off the TV or pause the channel, look in your spouse's eyes, and attentively listen to her. Your action in this scenario shows that you are emotionally intelligent and caring. You indirectly demonstrate that your spouse is more important to you than watching your favorite hockey team competition, and doing so has a heart-touching effect on your spouse's psyche. Being insensitive to your partner's emotional needs is a turn-off for a loving relationship. Men's brains are wired for problem-solving; thus, men should work on becoming more emotionally intelligent and responding empathetically to their woman's feelings. Men have developed characteristics to survive in harshness and provide for their families in a rough environment. What men need when treating their partner is kindness and gentleness. Even when a woman is serious, in her profound being is femininity, kindness, and compassion. If you are a man, learn to treat your partner always with tenderness to touch her soul.

Be Creative in Giving Gifts

The story of Darren Hardy's gift to his wife is inspiring. On one Thanksgiving Day, Darren Hardy, *The New York Times* best-selling author of *The Compound Effect,* decided to keep a diary, journaling for an entire year about his wife's positive qualities and behavior. Every day, he wrote for almost five minutes about what he could find regarding his wife's contributions to his life, and he felt gratitude for her presence and contributions. He wrote about how well she treated her friends, how she made delicious meals, how beautifully she styled her hair, how well she took care of family dogs, etc. He secretly kept writing the journal for a year, and on Thanksgiving Day, he gave the gratitude journal to his wife. When he gave the journal to his wife, it brought tears to her eyes. His wife told him that the gratitude journal was the best gift she had ever received. Hardy mentioned that by writing the daily gratitude journal, he could see the subtleties in his wife's nature and behavior instead of his wife's more obvious qualities. He forced himself to find more positive aspects of his wife and become more conscious of the beauties in her behavior and character that otherwise would not be noticed and appreciated. He said that his love life after giving the gratitude journal to his wife got better. The gift not only surprised his wife but also helped Hardy improve his ability to be more conscious in his relationship.

There are a few lessons to learn from Hardy's story. First, yearlong journaling and writing about his wife's positive qualities and behavior shows that he cares about his relationship and his wife. The daily repetition of Darren's positive behavior in writing the gratitude journal became so powerful that it brought tears to his wife's eyes. Second, your relationship needs your attention and time to foster and flourish. You should assign some time to nourish your relationship continuously. Third, a touching gift doesn't need to be expensive but should reflect that you care. For example, if you get flowers for your partner often, you can think about a creative way instead to convey the message of how important your partner is in your life. The time you spend making a gift and the pure attention you pay to getting a gift for your partner is louder than a thousand words.

Be Romantic for a Thriving Relationship

Though men may seem less romantic than women, men also want romance in their relationships. Being romantic is a personal trait; a man can be more romantic than a woman and vice versa. Inside all humans, there is love, but in some humans, love has been buried under their environmental programming and life experiences. Perhaps they have had some pitfalls in their early relationships and concluded that love does not exist, closing them off to any possible loving relationships. Deep inside every person, there is a longing for love and romance, and it has been so throughout history and among all cultures. Love has been the inspiring spirit for the world's masterpieces of literature and art. Romance is what makes a relationship beautiful and enjoyable. In past generations, women's expectations from their man were usually limited to providing food, shelter, and security. Women often were financially dependent on their man, and if a man could provide them and their children with the necessities for life, they would be satisfied. Romance was perceived as a luxury in tales and stories; some people even viewed romance as illogical. Things have changed now. Women and men want a high-quality relationship and romance. Many women have become financially independent. With respect to physiology, romance produces oxytocin in women's bodies, which helps them reduce their stress hormones and feel good. Having romance is not a luxury; it is a powerful way to enjoy life, feel good, and manage stress. Oxytocin is a binding hormone and prepares the body and mind for connection. If you have kids, having a romantic relationship with your partner conveys the message of love to your kids and prepares them for their future quality relationships. The energy of love, like other emotions, is contagious. Perhaps the best gift you can give your children is to have a romantic relationship with your partner so that they can learn what to expect from a relationship. Allocating time during the week to have romantic time with your partner is pivotal for your relationship to thrive.

Follow Your Dreams, Value Your Partner's Dreams, and Support Each Other

A purpose in life gives meaning to our existence. Share your deepest hopes and dreams with the closest human to you: your partner. You should feel safe and trust your partner to share your dreams and hopes that might not seem reachable or mentally acceptable. When listening to your partner's dreams and hopes, do not judge or express disappointing statements such as casting doubt on the feasibility and practicality of fulfilling their hopes and dreams; rather, demonstrate genuine curiosity and ask questions to know more about your partner's dreams, hopes, and life purpose.

The underlying conflict in your relationship may be an unfulfilled desire or life purpose. Maybe your partner unconsciously feels that she has been confined in the relationship and thus can't fulfill her life purpose. But when you lovingly become close to your partner to know her deepest desires and dreams, you know your partner at a deeper level than you have known so far. Dreaming together brings you both closer than ever. Support your partner on the journey toward her life purpose and dreams. You should also know your own life purpose and dreams. Knowing one's life purpose requires much inner work, leading to self-exploration and self-awareness. Many people don't know their life purpose; however when some people figure it out, they step closer toward fulfilling their mission in life. Living your life purpose and supporting each other on your path is a beautiful journey of love.

In a loving relationship, you are not just in love with your partner's personality and character or physical attraction but also with your partner's dreams, hopes, and life purpose. Talking about each other's life dreams and purpose can also be a great way of getting to know one another and becoming closer. Be part of each other's dreams and life purpose, and support each other on the journey of fulfilling a meaningful life. Let true love be your light and lead you in life.

Write down below the key points you learned in Chapter 8.

Chapter 9

The Spiritual Aspects of Your Relationship

Psychology is the study of humans' inner worlds based on visible and tangible information, whereas spirituality is the experience of discovering the inner world through an inner journey and personal reflection.

Some prominent psychologists and psychiatrists have acknowledged the importance of addressing the spiritual aspects of human issues and have begun using spiritual principles to solve complex inner-world problems.

Spiritual masters accentuate that the biggest enemy of humans is inside them: their mind or ego. The mind doesn't want change and growth; it does everything it can to keep the current situation unchanged. At the conscious level, you desire something heartedly, but at the subconscious level, there is resistance to change and fulfillment of your desire. You want true love, but the subconscious mind is unfamiliar with love, so it resists love and uses all kinds of sneaky tricks to keep the current situation *loveless*.

In spirituality, a relationship is beyond the connection between two humans; a relationship is a start for *union* with the entire being. In the relationship with your partner, you are learning to forget your *self* and become *one* with your partner. But you are not going to stop there; you will expand your union and love for more things and humans. In union with your partner, you become a channel through which the Infinite Love spreads love and light on planet Earth. So, spirituality has a much broader horizon for a relationship. You don't need to be spiritual to use spiritual views and solutions to help you grow and flourish in love and relationships. Whatever school of thought can help you effectively solve your problem without harming yourself or others should be welcome. The goal of any school of thought should be solving problems, growing in humanity, and welcoming life, not disputing who is right and who is wrong. Below are five pillars of spirituality based on Rumi's and other spiritual masters' teachings that can help you develop a loving relationship.

1. Genuine Gratitude

In spirituality, bad incidents don't exist. Everything happening in our outside world is mirroring our inner world. If the incident doesn't favor us, or we perceive it as undesired or even hurtful, it is a message to us so that we know something inside us needs to be cared for and healed. The incident did not occur by accident to injure us; it happened to awaken us to some inner unsolved problems that should be addressed. So, in spirituality, gratitude is not only for good things in life but also for unfavorable incidents that occur to awaken us to spiritual growth. From a spiritual perspective, inside any adversity, there is an opportunity for growth. Imagine when your partner does something that seems careless and faulty, but you realize something within yourself that has provoked that behavior.

Your partner was the mirror of your inner world so that you could see what was happening inside you. Shouldn't you thank your partner for helping you to unearth something hidden inside you that needs your care and should be healed? I understand that this perspective might be difficult for some people to grasp; however, it is a practical way that can yield a stunning breakthrough in your relationship. When you have a progressive, thankful heart, you see that everything happening in your life is occurring to serve you. The more you grow in spirituality, the more you understand that your relationship has a hidden purpose: to help you discover your childhood and adulthood wounds and resolve your unsolved emotional blockages inside you. Don't you think you should thank your partner for showing your inner wounds and making you aware of them? A spiritually advanced individual is always thankful because she perceives and is sure that everything is happening to serve her.

2. Acceptance

When facing an undesired incident in our relationship or misbehavior from our partner, we usually react quickly without much conscious mind attention. In spirituality, there is a moment of pure acceptance when an undesired incident and misbehavior happens. You just accept whatever it is without judgment and prejudice. You observe the situation, do not react, and let it pass through you without your mental resistance. When you don't react and don't judge the situation or your partner's misbehavior, you shut down your ego; that is a spiritual victory for you. Acceptance is one of the pillars of the spiritual journey. You don't let the external stimuli create a storm inside your inner ocean with a non-resistant attitude. *You can develop a mental attitude of equanimity and, in seemingly adverse situations, make acceptance your first response to the adversity.*

3. Self-Restraint

If a conflict arises in your relationship, your mind wants you to react quickly to the situation. For example, your partner may say something that hurts you, and you feel humiliated and insulted. Your mind quickly has a solution for you: to counterattack and say something to humiliate and insult your partner. That is the ego solution, adding more darkness to the darkness. Life is testing you through conflicts whether you say *yes* to light or darkness. Self-restraint means you say *no* to the solutions your old programming or ego is telling you to do in difficult situations. It is easy to follow the old programming solutions, and it is usually effortless, whereas self-restraint is difficult and somewhat painful. But when you say *no* to the ego and tolerate the initial pain, you gradually free yourself from the prison of the old programming and open up to light and peace. You respond to the situation from the love within and shed light on your relationship. Self-restraint also means self-regulation. To regulate your emotions, you should first become conscious of your thoughts, feelings, and reactions and then deliberately choose different thoughts, feelings, and responses.

4. Forbearance

When you want to practice self-restraint, you should have forbearance. Forbearance and patience go hand in hand. When facing difficult people in life, we should have forbearance and be patient. When you develop forbearance, you are confident that the sun will rise despite gloomy conditions, that difficulties are fleeting, and that, eventually, light overcomes darkness. When you know that, in the end, things will turn out to be good or even fantastic, you have more peace, and forbearance is easier to maintain.

5. Contentment

Contentment is the sweet spot of happiness in life. When you are content with yourself, others, your environment, and your relationship, you are in a state of peaceful happiness. You are content because you are at peace with everyone and everything in life. You are in harmony with life and flowing with it. You don't resist nor fight anything or anyone. The fruit of the four other pillars of spirituality is contentment. You practice gratitude to notice that no one and nothing is against you, and everything in the universe is working toward evolution, advancement, perfection, and harmony. You stay content even when things seem unfavorable and malefic. You accept whatever it is and do not judge or react because you are content, and you know, ultimately, everything will be alright. You practice self-restraint because you know there is a better way to spread light. With patience and forbearance, you open up your heart to light and let love within you respond in a loving manner.

The Mind Trick to Be Aware Of

The mind has a fake interpretation of spirituality. The mind may say that being patient in spirituality means inaction and tolerance. It is not true. In spirituality, you don't react and don't follow what your old programming wants you to do in a hurry. With genuine gratitude, acceptance, forbearance, self-restraint, and contentment, you let your inner love give you a loving solution, and you respond to the unfavorable situation beautifully to shed light on your relationship. I understand that it is not easy to harness the old programming and the ego. Still, you can attain a higher level of human growth through your mindful practice and willingness to grow in humanity and spirituality. When an adversity or a conflict occurs in your relationship, ask yourself these questions before any reaction:

Am I practicing genuine gratitude?
Am I accepting the situation without judgment, prejudice, and resistance?
Am I practicing patience and forbearance when responding to this situation?
Am I practicing self-restraint, not following my old programming's reaction to the situation?
Am I staying in peace and contentment?
What would be a loving response to this situation?

By answering these questions before any automatic reaction, you can control your impulsive behavior that might be destructive and respond constructively to the undesired situation.

Be an Observant of Your Feelings, Thoughts, and Behavior

Emotional behavior is mostly unconscious reactions to stimuli. In a conscious relationship, you want to become more conscious about your inner world, feelings and thoughts, and those of your partner. The more you know about your inner world and your partner's inner world, the better you can direct your relationship on the path of growth. A practical skill for becoming more aware of emotions and thoughts is to practice being observant of your thoughts, feelings, and behavior and being in the present moment.

To update your old programming and harness your mind, you should first become aware of your feelings, thoughts, and behavior. The subconscious mind is involved in all reactions and feelings we experience, which are automatic. Before any mental reaction, an external trigger activates the value system in the mind. The mind gives a value of good or bad to the trigger based on memories and experiences of the past. Then, the neural circuits are activated accordingly, and feelings emerge. In a relationship, a trigger activates the attachment style in the subconscious mind; everything happens in a fraction of a second. It is easy to follow what the subconscious mind is running, as it doesn't require conscious attention. If you want to take control of your subconscious mind programming, one effective strategy is to be observant of your feelings, thoughts, and behavior. You can practice imagining yourself from the outside as a third person and observe your inner world. There are some key points to follow when you are observing yourself. You shouldn't judge or resist your thoughts and feelings. You just observe them and let them pass without judgment or resistance. You want to become aware of their existence. After you become aware of what your subconscious programming is doing, you can write down:

What is the external trigger?
What are my thoughts regarding the trigger?
What are my emotions related to the trigger?
How am I feeling right now?
What is my reaction to the trigger?
What would be a better response to the trigger?
How would I add some dose of love to my response?

Reflection: The Gate to Self-Awareness

One of the extraordinary functions of the brain and human mind is *metacognition*, which simply means "thinking about thinking." Humans are the only creatures that can think and reflect on their past experiences, thoughts, and behaviors. Reflection on our thoughts and behaviors enables us to become aware of our destructive and constructive behaviors in a relationship and deliberately regulate our emotions in response to a stimulus. Studies have shown that parents with insecure attachment style can reflect on their connection experience with their primary caregivers when they were children and choose to be responsive to their offspring's emotional and physical needs, fostering children with secure attachment style. If parents were not self-reflective, they would treat their children according to autonomous mental models that they learned from their primary caregivers, fostering children with insecure attachment style. Truly reflecting on our thoughts and behaviors is an opening to self-awareness and constructive change in life. Without self-awareness, we become a tool for the automatic programs of the subconscious mind. Through self-awareness and new actions, we can create the life we want; otherwise, life happens to us.

Connection of Two States of Minds

The quality of a human's life is better determined by the quality of his states of mind. A state of mind at every moment includes beliefs, perceptions, intentions, feelings, desires, goals, attitudes, memories, and thoughts. A quality state of mind is calm and at peace; serenity is its normal attitude to external stimuli. In a loving relationship, the state of mind of one human is attuned with that of another human; the connection is at the subconscious level, and thus the conscious mind can't often explain why we love someone.

A loving relationship is a connection between two minds to form a channel through which their energy flows smoothly. Humans naturally seek connection. Studies in children's development show that the idea of a unitary *self* is an illusion the mind tries to make. We feel more whole when we relate to others, and the states of our mind exchange energy and information with the states of mind of others. We feel closer and more connected when we share similar beliefs, perceptions, goals, desires, and thoughts with other humans.

The states of mind of two lovers soothe each other. They make an invisible connection of unity in their field of energy. The well-being of another human becomes the well-being of oneself. There is no more *I* and *you*. Instead, there is *we*; there is *oneness*. The state of mind of two lovers in a relationship, at each moment, should be *one* state of mind. We may be conscious or unconscious about the state of our mind at each moment. Consciousness about the state of our mind is an opening to self-awareness and changing the quality of mind. For example, if you feel that you are bored in your relationship and become conscious that the state of your mind is sluggishness and boredom, you can change the state of your mind by remembering good memories of past exhilarating experiences or begin to plan for adventuring with your partner to change the state of your mind immediately.

There are many ways to enhance the quality of your mind at each moment, among which are gratitude, positivity, hopefulness, trusting, caring, liking, loving, self-love, self-compassion, respectfulness, forgiving, anticipating a desired outcome, remembering a good event in the past, and the like. A state of mind at each moment is transmissible, meaning when you are in a state of gratitude, you emit the energy and information of gratitude vibe to people around you and create a positive energy field. Your state of mind affects your nonverbal communication, such as facial expression, body language, and eye contact, and conveys good energy to people around you. The state of mind mostly affects those who are physically and emotionally close to you. For example, a mother's state of mind directly affects her children's state of mind. An anxious mother triggers anxiety for her children's state of mind. Because children are very suggestible, they are much more sensitive and prone to be influenced by others' states of mind, especially their primary caregivers.

In your relationship, your state of mind shapes the quality of your relationship and is transmissible. By working on yourself and enhancing the quality of your mind, you can enhance the quality of your partner's mind and improve your relationship. People often look for the best brands for their clothes, cars, and other material things. I don't judge that, but the most important possession one can have at a given moment is a quality state of mind, so it is better to look for the quality state of mind before other things. Pay attention to the fact that the quality of mind exists only in the present moment. So, at each moment, the state of mind can change. By developing a positive mental attitude, we can often maintain a quality state of mind and transmit good energy and positivity to our relationship and connection with our beloved. When your mind is attuned to the state of mind of your partner, your relationship is in harmony.

The Ego Makes Illusions to Hinder a Loving Relationship

No other human, including your partner, knows your thoughts. But the energy of your thoughts has a direct effect on your relationship. People who are truly committed to their partner don't think even for a second that their ideal partner is somewhere else, and they do not fantasize about being with another fantasy or real person who is superior to their current flawed partner. In their mind, there is no place for a fantasy or real person who has been idealized and who fulfills all their unmet desires, emotional intimacies, and sexual fantasies. They do not hesitate about whether their partner is the right person to be with. They never threaten their partner to leave because threatening cultivates the seed of insecurity and mistrust in their relationship. They have made up their mind to be in a committed relationship to learn and grow together. If your partner has flaws, you have flaws as well. We are all humans with good qualities and flaws. However, the ego is not humble enough to accept having flaws. If you are still thinking that another person will be your ideal partner somewhere out there and have not made up your mind to truly commit to your partner mentally, emotionally, and physically, I highly recommend you do the three Golden Exercises at the end of this book. Because being fully committed to a partner is at the core of developing a loving relationship. So, you want to build your loving relationship on a robust foundation. I emphasize that the development of a loving relationship is absolutely possible when you know that your ego and conditioned mind are playing games with you to hinder you from a genuine connection with your partner; the playfield is inside your mind.

Life is a mind game; the better you know how to play the life game, the better you live. You should know that, from the spiritual perspective, you are tested with what you've got. Are you grateful for what you have got? Are you content with what you have created? Or do you fall into the mind trap of comparing your partner with others or questioning your partner's worthiness for a relationship? Answering these questions and reflecting on your answers can help you know why your relationship does not improve and goes nowhere. I am not talking about abusive or violent relationships; if you are in such a relationship, take the necessary steps and get advice from professional couples therapists.

Comparison Hurts Your Relationship

One of the mental attitudes is comparison. This mental ability is useful when we decide what to choose in our day-to-day life. For example, we go to a grocery store and see a product is on sale; we compare the price of the item with the same product in the other grocery store and understand the price is considerably lower, and so we decide to buy the product. You see that comparison is a useful mental tool when it is used where it should be used. Nevertheless, using the comparison faculty in a relationship can heavily hurt your relationship. This is because the relationship is a convoluted connection with another human being, a connection between two inner worlds that are mostly unknown even to oneself; there needs to be much more information to compare your partner with anyone else, and, usually, we can't access all information to compare properly.

From the spiritual perspective, the mind or ego always looks for short-term gratifications and overlooks their detrimental consequences. The ego is against you. If you compare your partner with your ex and maximize the good traits of your ex to belittle your partner in your mind, you have fallen into a mind trap that is stealing your happiness.

If you compare your partner with movie stars and beautiful people you meet in the street, you are unconsciously ruining your relationship. Nothing is enough for the ego. If you marry the most attractive person in the world, I promise that if you follow your ego and compare your spouse with others, soon you will begin to want to be with someone else. Though you might not act, your comparison and the egoistic desire in your mind negatively affect your relationship, hindering a loving connection with your partner. The ego abuses the comparison faculty of your mind, and you shouldn't let it do so.

Comparing your partner with others is usually a thinking error. The mind positively filters other people's looks or exaggerates their good traits while discounting or ignoring your partner's good qualities. I highly recommend that you set a rule and prohibit any mental comparison of your partner with your exes or anyone else.

Say *Yes* to the Light

Deep inside our being, we usually know what is right or wrong. We know telling the truth is right and lying is wrong; why? Because we don't want to be lied to. We know commitment in a relationship is the right thing to do; why? Because we don't want to be cheated on. We know that treating our partner with respect is the right thing to do because we want to be treated with respect. There is always programming that induces reactive behavior that would be destructive to the relationship. We should train our minds to control it and learn to say *yes* to what we already know is the right thing to do. We should say *yes* to the light and say *no* to the darkness. Self-interests can blind us to our partner's interests. When you choose to say *yes* to the light, even when your partner is saying *yes* to the darkness, you emanate light to the relationship.

The main point here is that you do so merely for the sake of doing what is right without any expectations from your partner. You say *yes* to the light because you cherish goodness and fairness. There is always a challenge inside humans: to choose the right thought and respond properly or to choose the wrong thought and react impulsively. Saying *yes* to the light may be painful for your ego; nevertheless, act fairly and rightly. Let your ego go through suffering and a new version of you reborn. It is hard when your partner lies to you, but you choose not to get angry; instead, do something good for your partner and calmly tell your partner that you don't accept lies and expect him to be trustworthy. If you insist on staying with the light and don't compromise goodness, your partner either responds with light to your relationship and adapts to your light energy or will go out of your life, and someone who is aligned with your energy will beautifully enter your life. But remember, we cannot expect our partner to treat us with fairness and respect while we, mentally or through our behavior, don't treat him rightly in harmony with the light. We should work on ourselves and do our best to say *yes* to the light in our relationship as much as we can without any expectations from our partner.

The Spiritual Perspective on Individual Attachment Style

When we were born and came to Earth, we were pure beings full of love, without judgment and blame, without feeling superior to others, without grudge, and without feeling inferior, unloved, or unworthy. We were designed to love; we were full of life, ready to connect with our environment and people who were close to us. We tried to connect with our primary caregivers (often parents) through eye contact and touching. Connection with others meant our survival. Some of us could receive appropriate care and response to our connection needs, and some of us received inadequate care and were neglected. Now, our pure being is receiving new data from the environment, and we are adapting to the situation in which we live. The new data shapes our brain and covers our core being, which is love, with mental models that are meant to work in the physical dimension for connection with others. The mental models represent the ego of each individual. If we receive love and care from our primary caregivers who are responsive and available to our emotional and physical needs, we receive love added to our pure being. We develop a healthy attachment style through which we connect with others, including our partner, in a healthy and loving way. If our primary caregivers are not loving and do not respond to our emotional and physical needs in a timely manner and are neglectful, our pure being does not receive love, and the data from the environment builds a coverage over our pure being. The substance of this coverage is not from love but neglect, indifference, and insecurity. The veil made from indifference is built by the ego. To develop a secure attachment, we should overcome what our ego wants.

For some people with an avoidant attachment style, the ego views the other person in a relationship as inferior and sees itself as superior so that a healthy connection cannot be established. Some people with an anxious attachment style perceive themselves as inferior and their partner as superior and idealize their partner or the one they are attracted to. Any feeling of superiority or inferiority is from the ego, which does not reflect the reality of who we are, which is pure love. The ego wants to judge others; it blames others for problems and believes that it has no flaws, and it thinks it knows everything, so it doesn't want to learn and advance. When you accept your role in a conflict in your relationship, you become humble and pass over your ego. You become open to change and improvement. Any conflict in a relationship is a conflict between two egos. The pure essence inside you and your partner does not have any problem with each other; they are one; they are love. The ego always looks for ease and comfort, while growth asks for movement and facing challenges. In developing a secure attachment style, you should know that what is resisting inside you is your ego, the programming you received from others, covering your pure essence of love. In developing a secure attachment, you should avoid strategies the ego uses to protect itself from change and growth. Some of the strategies used by the ego are mentioned below:

- Blaming others and yourself
- Judging and prejudice
- Believing that it knows what to do, so it is not open to learning and growth
- Moving you to the worries of the future as well as the sadness and regret in the past to steal from you the present moment

By applying spiritual principles, you become humble and accept that there are some inner issues that you want to address. You don't even resist their presence. You just observe and accept them without judgment and let them pass inside you. When you become more self-aware, you begin to realize that the biggest obstacles hindering you from growing in life reside inside yourself. Here is a quote by Rumi that would help you understand how you can progress in life:

> Consult with your ego in affairs of life,
> Whatever it says, its opposite is integrity and
> sublimation.

So, when there is a dispute between you and your partner, you should know that, from a spiritual standpoint, you are not in dispute; your ego and your partner's ego are arguing; ask your ego what it advises you to do and then do the opposite.

Turning from *Self* toward the Significant *Other*

When entering the vibe of love, the attention turns from the *self* to the other being, making the self less important than it was before. Self-interests pale, and the beloved's interests stand out. The questions that a true lover asks his beloved are like these:

How can I express my love to you?
How can I bring more peace into your life?
How can I help you to grow and flourish in life?
How can I make you happier?

When one's mindset shifts from "What can I *get* in my relationship?" to "What can I *give* in my relationship?" and actively wants to contribute to the relationship, the path to welcoming true love opens.

In most relationship problems, one or both persons actively think about their wants and needs. Though these wants and needs might seem reasonable, they lack the fundamental requirement for true love: actively thinking about the other person's needs and wants and putting the *self's* needs and wants aside. When two people in a relationship actively think about giving to one another, then being in that relationship feels like paradise on Earth.

Relationship books often recommend that couples look for mutual interests rather than self-interests. Doing so is a big step toward developing a loving relationship. However, those who look for an advanced level of a loving relationship should look for their beloved's interests. One may say, "Isn't that ignoring the self? Isn't that devastating to self-esteem and self-confidence?" To answer this question, I say that when a person has reached a high level of loving personality, she has evolved within and developed a strong, advanced human character. She is so filled with love inside that she wants to give; the more she loves, the more she receives love from within. The feeling of self-ignoring in a loving relationship comes from perceiving a relationship as a trade: I give something to you, and, in return, you give me back something.

In a loving relationship, you give because you are overwhelmed with goodness and want to share your good feelings of love. So, the more you give, the more self-esteem and self-confidence you have. You don't receive something from the outside to fill the emptiness within. You are full of love and want to share it without expectations.

Soften Heart

When you fall in love, your heart becomes soft, your mental barriers fall away, and you let the energy of another human enter your deepest existence. The risk of falling in love is whether you can establish a reliable connection with your beloved. You become flexible; you take the risk wholeheartedly. A softened heart makes room for emotional connection and expands you beyond *self*. When your heart is soft, you don't follow your old programming because it is not as rigid as it was before. A situation that would make you angry before does not bother you anymore, as your beloved is with you, though she might have been involved in making the situation. The old saying, "Whatever comes from the beloved is pleasing," makes sense. The shoulds and shouldn'ts have become less important. Love is an opportunity to change and grow because your heart has softened. Your heart is filled with mercy and compassion.

A rigid heart is closed and inflexible; it is hard like a piece of stone, closed to any emotional connection. Having a softened heart is so vital for the soul that Rumi prayed for others to have a softened heart. To connect with others, we should be open to receiving kindness from others and interpret their kindness optimistically. It can be challenging to make your heart softer if you have had problematic experiences in trusting others. The human mind's primary goal is survival, and past experiences are strong evidence of how to deal with life so that we are protected. But most of the time, this protection mechanism is out of proportion, especially if you are already in a relationship. The mental barriers to the emotional connection with your partner imprison your heart, blocking your connection with your partner. Be open to giving and receiving acts of kindness; some people are good givers but have trouble receiving. Accept your partner's desire for closeness and embrace vulnerability. You don't need to listen to your old programming in your subconscious mind that wants to protect you and use outdated data for your current connection. You may feel anxious when you want to be soft and let your partner enter your heart; it is natural, as it is a new experience for you, and you are stepping on a path of ambiguity and unfamiliarity. Endure the anxiety and overcome your fear of closeness and openness. Your anxiety is from the fear of intimacy and vulnerability. When you continue to take action despite your fear and gradually open up your heart for closeness, your anxiety will vanish, and the feelings of exhilaration and intimacy will follow. Your heart becomes soft; you become connected. Always remind yourself how you can overcome your rigid heart and unearth your true essence, which is pure love. Think about the concept of a softened heart and reflect on how you can have a softer heart in your relationship and how it can help you be closer to your partner.

From Conscious Mind to Conscious Relationship

One of the most crucial skills a human can acquire to direct thoughts and prosper in life is the ability to harness mental energy and thoughts. An untrained mind is restive, wandering in an unknown future and inaccessible past or dwelling in an unwanted present. Thinking about the future with fear causes anxiety, and ruminating about a gloomy past makes people depressed. Perceiving the current situation as undesired and unwanted leaves people frustrated and angry. But how can one harness thoughts? The ability to control your thoughts is an invaluable skill and is learnable. For thousands of years, religions have taught humans how to use certain words, affirmations, prayers, and rosaries to control the mind and direct the mental energy to positivity. In Eastern religions, meditation and yoga have been used to calm down the mind and make it more peaceful. There might be other ways to help you control your thoughts and mental energy that suits you the best. Some people may go to nature and pay meticulous attention to the natural beauties and wildlife. Others may use art as a way to calm down and stay peaceful.

A simple yet effective way to learn and develop consciousness of the self and of the world is to pay more attention to the inputs of your five senses and direct your thoughts toward experiencing the world through the five senses. For example, let's say you want to eat an apple. Conscious eating is first to carefully look at the apple and notice its color, shape, and size; then, you touch the apple and feel its size, shape, and all its details; next, you smell it; and finally you eat the apple and feel the sensation of the apple on your lips, teeth, and inside your mouth. Listen to the sound of your eating. You pay attention only to the taste of the apple and all that you are experiencing through your five senses. You keep your thoughts on the activity that you are doing and enjoy eating the apple slowly to the fullest. You will notice how much more delicious the apple is when you are conscious of eating it. When you slow down and pay careful attention to what you do, you take control over your automatic subconscious mind while doing your work and consciously observe, listen, touch, smell, and taste. When you mindfully do things that have been done so far through your subconscious mind, you connect to the present moment where life is flowing. You direct your thoughts from the past and future toward the eternal present.

Developing a conscious mind is the first step toward a conscious relationship. When you are with your partner listening to her, you should stay in the present moment, even for five minutes every day. You should use some of your five senses to connect with your partner. Look at her eyes with tenderness, hold her hands, and feel the sensation of her hands on your hand and their warmth or coldness; listen attentively with your heart to what she is telling you and express your empathy. Do not let your thoughts go to the past or the future. Do not let anything disturb your connection time. Everything else, except the present moment, is only memory and, in reality, doesn't exist anymore. When you become more conscious about your partner's presence and her concerns and feelings, you will notice that you are closer to each other than before. When you become more conscious of your partner, you will enjoy her companionship at a higher level. You shed light on your relationship, and in response to your higher consciousness, she also sheds light on your connection; thus, you will experience a more meaningful relationship and deeper connection.

The subconscious mind works very fast and frees the conscious mind for other important tasks in life. For example, your heartbeat and breathing are done by the subconscious mind. Imagine you needed to use your conscious mind for breathing or your heart functioning; that would be an end to life. But your relationship needs your mindful attention to grow and flourish. The subconscious mind uses the attachment style programming that you have learned mostly during your childhood and adulthood experiences in connection with others. If your relationship has some problems and is not as good as it should be, you should use a conscious relationship approach to direct your relationship, not letting your subconscious mind hurt your connection with your partner with its deflective attachment programming. The Golden Exercise.2 and Golden Exercise.3 in the Appendix can help you develop conscious relationship skills. You can also deliberate and discover how you can stay in the present moment with your partner to enjoy your partner's companionship.

Forgive and Apologize

A mature human apologizes when he makes mistakes and asks for forgiveness if his actions hurt others or their feelings. The first strategy that the ego uses when making a mistake is not to accept the mistake and deny it. However, there is a *higher self* within that knows what is right and what is wrong, and we should listen to that higher self. Even when you feel that you are right in a conflict with your partner, if you hurt your partner's feelings and make her feel down and miserable, you are doing something wrong. Have the courage to be responsible and accountable when you make mistakes, listen to your higher self, and profusely apologize and ask for forgiveness. After making a mistake in your relationship, if you don't follow your ego and become humble to apologize and ask for forgiveness, you bring out the higher self of your partner and feel a close connection between you. When it is right, apologizing and asking for forgiveness are among the greatest human attributes. When you forgive a mistake, you shouldn't feel morally superior because you do yourself a favor, not your partner; you free yourself from the burden of reaction through anger, grudges, sadness, envy, or other low-vibration feelings. Forgiveness is saying *yes* to the light and *no* to the automatic reaction; forgiveness is a response, not a reaction to a mistake; forgiveness is an update for your old programming in your subconscious mind. Your old programming might feel uncomfortable when you want to forgive, but you should convince yourself through constructive self-talk that forgiveness is the best option for you, your partner, and your relationship.

Let's say your partner has made a mistake that is clearly his fault. That means the mistake has spread darkness in the relationship. What would be the reasonable response to darkness? Is the solution adding more darkness to the problem or adding more light? If you follow your old programming and react when your partner has made a mistake, you most likely add more darkness to an already dark situation, whereas your relationship needs you to shed light on your relationship.

Forgiveness is learnable. Because we have not been taught enough about forgiveness, we don't remember to use it when needed. The art of a loving relationship is also to forgive and compromise. One of the main attributes of people with a secure attachment style is that they are quick in forgiving; when their partner makes a mistake, they don't ruminate over it for days and keep it in their explicit memory.

Forgive Those Who Have Programmed You with the Insecure Attachment Style

Your current relationship is based on the mental model you developed through your early communications with your primary caregivers, who were most likely your parents. If you have an insecure attachment style, struggle to have a loving relationship, and have difficulties connecting with other humans, you might feel angry and frustrated toward your parents or primary caregivers. You may feel grudges and hatred in your heart, keeping the frightening feelings of unmet needs and neglected emotional wants. But you no longer need to carry the burden of heavy feelings. Forgiveness of your parents or primary caregivers frees you from stuck emotions. Let go of old feelings and feel the freedom from your past experiences. Your parents have had their inner emotional wounds and unconsciously were unresponsive, negligent, or inconsistent in responding to your physical and emotional needs. Understand your primary caregivers and forgive them. Forgiveness needs some inner work, and it might take some time, but your willingness to forgive your parents or primary caregivers is the first step. You should convince yourself that your parents did what they could based on their understanding and level of consciousness, and how they treated you had nothing to do with you personally.

You may also need to forgive your ex. People often unknowingly run the programs they have received from others; unless they become conscious and willing to change their destructive behavior, they run others' programming installed inside them. Indeed, forgiving others is a gift to yourself and a gate to emotional freedom.

I will share my relationship with my father with you. In my experience, my father was emotionally the coldest human I have ever seen. He was not rude, aggressive, or violent, but his silence was scary. I always wanted to connect with him and get his attention and love, but I was never successful. I felt resentful and angry. I could not understand why my father was so cold and indifferent. I lost my father in a car accident when I was fourteen years old, and I never received love from him. His loss was heavy on my shoulders. Even after my father passed away, I had an ironic, unconscious mixture of resentment and love in my heart for him. There was a tightness around my chest and neck and an emotional blockage, but I was not aware of its cause. The memory of my father during my childhood was painful. When I was in my thirties, I became aware of my deep resentment and grudge against my father and decided to forgive him. Forgiving him took some time, but eventually, I was released from the emotional blockage and tightness of my chest and neck.

Later on, when I studied different schools of psychology, I could understand why my father was emotionally so cold. He had lost his father when he was only four years old. He had not experienced a close connection with his father, so he did not know how to connect with his kids. My father's mental model for connection with others was deactivated, and he had an avoidant attachment style. He did not know how to love or be in touch with his buried emotional needs for connection. It was not his fault that I couldn't connect with him; it was his old programming running automatically in his subconscious mind that kept him emotionally distant even from his children. After I understood the root causes of my father's emotional distance and indifference, not only did I forgive him but I also felt a deep compassion for him. I perceive my father as a four-year-old kid who has lost his father and does not receive his father's love and attention, and I feel compassion toward him to this day. When you understand the ones toward whom you feel resentment, you can forgive them. Understanding and empathy are the key ingredients for forgiving and freeing yourself from hatred and resentment.

On your life journey with your partner, you may become aware that forgiveness is what you need the most. The concept of forgiveness is not only a moral value but an essential part of psychological health and human growth. You should learn to be quick in forgiveness; your partner is not your enemy; she is the closest human to you. Forgive your partner's mistakes quickly, forget about them, and remember all her good qualities.

Your Relationship Purpose and Personality Growth

A relationship may fulfill some basic human psychological and instinctive needs; nevertheless, in the bigger picture, it is for healing your emotional wounds, growth, and spiritual advancement. On the journey toward growing as a human being, you encounter obstacles. The ego's solution is to change your partner; that is the easiest way to solve the problem superficially because you do not need to change and leave your comfort zone. Though the ego's solutions for relationship problems might seem easy at first glimpse, they are costly in the long run, resulting in frustration and loneliness. You choose the easy way but end up suffering and in turmoil.

On the contrary, when you perceive your relationship problems as opportunities to solve and grow, you choose to be uncomfortable and step beyond your old programming and mental rules. Through self-reflection, you discover that you have a wall around your heart that prevents you from establishing a heart-to-heart connection with your partner. You begin to understand that you should develop empathy and understand your partner. You understand that your partner is a mirror reflecting your inner world. When you treat your partner with honesty, sincerity, and respect while practicing self-love and self-respect, in return, you receive honesty, sincerity, and respect from your partner. When you act in your relationship with responsibility and care, you uncover the light inside your partner's being and receive goodness in return. When you are grateful toward your partner and his contributions to your life, your energy emits positivity, and your partner receives your energy even though it is invisible.

Ironically, most people respect strangers more than they respect their dearest ones. Practice treating your partner and children with kindness. When you treat your partner with kindness in any situation, you cultivate a land of peace and love between you. Kindness is a trait of people with high moral standards. Try to be more generous; if your spouse or partner likes to receive gifts, give her gifts often and surprise her with your creativity. Your gift doesn't need to be expensive but should show that you have carefully made or chosen it.

Flexibility in a relationship is essential if you want minimum friction in your interactions with your partner. Every human has a way of doing things and is experiencing a different lifestyle; flexibility is the key to establishing a beautiful connection with others, particularly your partner.

Being loyal in your relationship builds trust between you. Trust is the foundation for a long-term relationship. On your relationship journey, be patient. Strive to become a better version of yourself and see how your partner responds to your personal growth accordingly. Every day, be a little kinder, a little more patient, a little more caring, a little more grateful, a little more flexible, a little more generous, a little more forgiving, and a little more loving, and see how your relationship gradually transforms to the best state possible.

The purpose of your relationship is to know yourself better, improve your good qualities, and amend your flaws to become a better human being. You should emigrate from *self* and expand within to be *one* with another human being. And the ultimate goal is to become *one* with everything in the Universe. There is no *me*, *you*, or *it*; there is *oneness*, and everything is connected. The capacity to care for everything begins with practicing the concept of *oneness* with your partner. We have seen an enormous capacity of loving in spiritual figures who have fallen in love with the entire creation. Though we are not saints or spiritual figures, we can demonstrate the concept of unconditional love to some extent with our beloved and with people we know. You have the capacity to grow and deserve to experience a life full of love, peace, health, and abundance. And reading this book proves that you want to grow and welcome love in your heart and relationship.

Write down below the key points you learned in Chapter 9.

Appendix

Golden Exercises

These three golden exercises have been designed to increase your consciousness and reprogram your mind for a close connection and quality relationship with your partner. Make sure to do them with commitment, persistence, love, and hope. Writing stimulates thinking, and repetitive reading of your writings creates new neural pathways and circuits in your brain to transform your mental patterns into a more constructive way of thinking and behavior. Your mind doesn't want you to change and uses a variety of tricks to dissuade you from doing the exercises for constructive changes. One of the mind tricks to prevent changes in your thought patterns and behavior is *forgetfulness*. Your mind wants you to forget to do the daily exercises; you must do your best to do the exercises every single day to develop new mental patterns and behaviors. Another trick the mind uses is telling you, "They are not going to work," to demoralize you from doing the exercises. Do not listen to your mind and persist in doing the exercises daily. Doing exercises every day conveys a powerful message to your subconscious mind that your relationship is crucial to you and that you are working to improve it; therefore, your subconscious mind will use all its resources and power to help you achieve your objectives regarding your relationship. Your mind may also want you to gather more information and read more books about relationships so that you don't take action. Be aware of the overpreparation mind trap and take action to change and advance in your life and relationship.

Studies show that, depending on the complexity of a task, building a new habit takes a few weeks to six months to form. Be patient when doing the daily mental exercises so you can thrive in your relationship and experience a higher level of love and intimacy. Refrain from judging the exercises, and be determined and persistent until the course of the exercise is over. You will be astonished by the result. *You must do the following three Golden Exercises for forty days without missing a day.* Use a table or calendar to record your daily practice. These mental exercises are powerful; don't let your mind resist your attempts to create a loving relationship with your partner. Your mind may say, "I'll do it later." However, commit to doing the exercises enthusiastically every day. You deserve love, and your striving and patience to experience a loving relationship will tremendously benefit your connection.

Golden Exercise. 1

Commitment and trust are the basis of a quality relationship. As discussed in the book, true commitment is to be loyal in your relationship in your mind, heart, imagination, and action. You must make up your mind that your partner is the best person for you on Earth to have a relationship with and be firmly committed to him or her even in your mind.

- First, write reasons why your partner is the best person on Earth for you to be with. If you need more space to write, use a separate sheet of paper to write more reasons; think as much as possible and write <u>at least ten reasons.</u>

1. ....

2. ....

3. ....

4. ....

5. ....

6. ....

7. ....

8. ....

9. ....

10. ....

- Using the reasons you listed above, write a script to convince yourself why your partner is the best person on Earth for *you* based on who you *are*. If, in your current relationship, you are not convinced that your partner is the best person for you to be in a relationship with, you must read the reasons you have mentioned above and your writing *for at least forty days without missing any day.* You should talk to yourself and read your writing to convince yourself that your partner is the best human for you to be in a relationship with and that you are faithful to him (her) mentally, emotionally, and physically.

....

....

....

....

....

....

....

....

....

....
....
....
....
....
....
....
....
....
....
....
....
....
....
....
....
....
....
....
....
....
....
....
....
....

Golden Exercise. 2

Throughout this exercise, you will train your mind to develop a thankful, appreciative attitude toward your partner. This exercise helps you not take your partner for granted. When you do this exercise, you train your mind to know your partner better, find beautiful qualities in him or her, and appreciate those qualities. By doing this exercise, you will feel better about your partner, which will positively affect your relationship. This exercise is powerful and effective. It takes some energy and time but do it anyway to create new neural pathways and circuits in your brain for connection and closeness to your partner.

- Write every day for ten days ten unique, good qualities pertinent to your partner's personality, character, behavior, physical attraction, capabilities, achievements, and skills. After each day, write down your genuine gratitude, admiration, and appreciation toward your partner based on the unique, good qualities you wrote on that day. All the one hundred unique, good qualities of your partner that you write during the first ten days of the exercise have to be distinct. Then, for forty more days, read twice a day what you have written during the first ten days for about ten to fifteen minutes and feel gratitude, admiration, and appreciation toward your partner.

- When doing the above exercise, at a certain point, you may find it hard to find more positive personal traits and good behaviors in your partner. It is a crucial time because by thinking and contemplation, you push your mind further to create new neural pathways and circuits, thus increasing your consciousness and expanding your perception's horizon of your partner's good qualities and positive behavior. So, be patient, think, and complete the exercise.

Day. 1

- Write down ten unique, good qualities of your partner:

1. ....

2. ....

3. ....

4. ....

5. ....

6. ....

7. ....

8. ....

9. ....

10. ....

- Now, write to express your gratitude, admiration, and appreciation toward your partner. Feel good and grateful when you write and read your expressions.

....

....

- Talk with yourself during the day about what you have written about your partner and feel good about him or her and your relationship.

Day. 2

- Write down ten unique, good qualities of your partner:

1. ....

2. ....

3. ....

4. ....

5. ....

6. ....

7. ....

8. ....

9. ....

10. ....

- Now, write to express your gratitude, admiration, and appreciation toward your partner. Feel good and grateful when you write and read your expressions.

....

....

- Talk with yourself during the day about what you have written about your partner and feel good about him or her and your relationship.

Day. 3

- Write down ten unique, good qualities of your partner:

1. ....

2. ....

3. ....

4. ....

5. ....

6. ....

7. ....

8. ....

9. ....

10. ....

- Now, write to express your gratitude, admiration, and appreciation toward your partner. Feel good and grateful when you write and read your expressions.

....

....

....

....

....

....

....

....

....

....

....

....

....

....

....

....

....

....

....

....

....

....

....

- Talk with yourself during the day about what you have written about your partner and feel good about him or her and your relationship.

Day. 4

- Write down ten unique, good qualities of your partner:

1. ....

2. ....

3. ....

4. ....

5. ....

6. ....

7. ....

8. ....

9. ....

10. ....

- Now, write to express your gratitude, admiration, and appreciation toward your partner. Feel good and grateful when you write and read your expressions.

....

....

- Talk with yourself during the day about what you have written about your partner and feel good about him or her and your relationship.

Day. 5

- Write down ten unique, good qualities of your partner:

1. ....

2. ....

3. ....

4. ....

5. ....

6. ....

7. ....

8. ....

9. ....

10. ....

- Now, write to express your gratitude, admiration, and appreciation toward your partner. Feel good and grateful when you write and read your expressions.

....

....

- Talk with yourself during the day about what you have written about your partner and feel good about him or her and your relationship.

Day. 6

- Write down ten unique, good qualities of your partner:

1. ....

2. ....

3. ....

4. ....

5. ....

6. ....

7. ....

8. ....

9. ....

10. ....

- Now, write to express your gratitude, admiration, and appreciation toward your partner. Feel good and grateful when you write and read your expressions.

....

....

....

....

....

....

....

....

....

....

....

....

....

....

....

....

....

....

....

....

....

....

....

- Talk with yourself during the day about what you have written about your partner and feel good about him or her and your relationship.

Day. 7

- Write down ten unique, good qualities of your partner:

1. ....

2. ....

3. ....

4. ....

5. ....

6. ....

7. ....

8. ....

9. ....

10. ....

- Now, write to express your gratitude, admiration, and appreciation toward your partner. Feel good and grateful when you write and read your expressions.

....

....

- Talk with yourself during the day about what you have written about your partner and feel good about him or her and your relationship.

Day. 8

- Write down ten unique, good qualities of your partner:

1. ....

2. ....

3. ....

4. ....

5. ....

6. ....

7. ....

8. ....

9. ....

10. ....

- Now, write to express your gratitude, admiration, and appreciation toward your partner. Feel good and grateful when you write and read your expressions.

....

....

- Talk with yourself during the day about what you have written about your partner and feel good about him or her and your relationship.

Day. 9

- Write down ten unique, good qualities of your partner:

1. ....

2. ....

3. ....

4. ....

5. ....

6. ....

7. ....

8. ....

9. ....

10. ....

- Now, write to express your gratitude, admiration, and appreciation toward your partner. Feel good and grateful when you write and read your expressions.

....

....

- Talk with yourself during the day about what you have written about your partner and feel good about him or her and your relationship.

Day. 10

- Write down ten unique, good qualities of your partner:

1. ....

2. ....

3. ....

4. ....

5. ....

6. ....

7. ....

8. ....

9. ....

10. ....

- Now, write to express your gratitude, admiration, and appreciation toward your partner. Feel good and grateful when you write and read your expressions.

....

....

- Talk with yourself during the day about what you have written about your partner and feel good about him or her and your relationship.

Golden Exercise. 3

In this exercise, you should express your gratitude and appreciation directly toward your partner daily for a few minutes. You can talk to your partner about his or her contribution to your life, good qualities, and personal characteristics. You can remember the good things your partner has done in the past and express gratitude. You can also use what you have written in Golden Exercise. 2 to express your good feelings to your partner. Continue Golden Exercise. 3 for forty days and record on a table or calendar to track your progress.

- The more you do the exercises, the easier they will become. The point is to enhance and upgrade your consciousness in your relationship. You may want to practice one of the exercises that has had the best effect on your relationship for another forty days or until it is ingrained in your subconscious mind and becomes part of your habitual thinking and behavior.

- Reread this book, highlight parts that you find helpful for your relationship, and apply the knowledge you have learned.

References

1. Quran
2. Burns, D. D. (1999). *Feeling Good: The New Mood Therapy.* Avon Books, NY, U.S.
3. Burns, D. D. (2020). *Feeling Great: The Revolutionary New Treatment for Depression and Anxiety.* PESI Publishing, WI, U.S.
4. Siegel, D. J. (1999). *The Developing Mind: How Relationships and the Brain Interact to Shape Who We Are.* Guilford Press, NY, U.S.
5. Frederick, R. J. (2019). *Loving Like You Mean It: Use the Power of Emotional Mindfulness to Rewire Your Brain and Transform Your Relationships.* Central Recovery Press, NV, U.S.
6. Maltz, M. (2015). *Psycho-Cybernetics.* Penguin Random House LLC, NY, U.S.
7. Beck, J. S. (2011). *Cognitive Behavior Therapy: Basics and Beyond.* Guilford Press, NY, U.S
8. Gottman, J. and Silver, N. (1999). *The Seven Principles for Making Marriage Work: A Practical Guide from the Country's Foremost Relationship Expert.* Harmony Books, NY, U.S.

9. Gottman, J., Gottman, J. S., Abrams, D., and Abrams, R. C. (2019). *Eight Dates: Essential Conversations for a Lifetime of Love.* Workman Publishing, NY, U.S.
10. Beck, A. T. (1989). *Love Is Never Enough: How Couples Can Overcome Misunderstandings, Resolve Conflicts, and Solve.* Harper Perennial, NY, U.S.
11. Hendrix, H. (2007). *Getting the Love You Want, 20th Anniversary Edition: A Guide for Couples.* St. Martin's Griffin, NY, U.S.
12. Levine, A. and Heller, R. (2012). *Attached: The New Science of Adult Attachment and How It Can Help You Find—and Keep—Love.* TarcherPerigee, NY, U.S.
13. Gray, J. (2020). *Beyond Mars and Venus: Relationship Skills for Today's Complex World.* BenBella Books, TX, U.S.
14. Goulston, M. and Goldberg, P. (2001). *The 6 Secrets of a Lasting Relationship: How to Fall in Love Again—and Stay There.* TarcherPerigee, NY, U.S.
15. Johnson, S. (2013). *Love Sense: The Revolutionary New Science of Romantic Relationships.* Little, Brown Spark, NY, U.S.
16. Lally, P., Pos, H. W. W., Van Jaarsveld, C. H. M., and Wardle, J. (2010). *How Are Habits Formed: Modelling Habit Formation in the Real World.* European Journal of Social Psychology, 40, 998-1009, London, U.K.

About the Author:

S. Morteza Lajevardi is the *Peace and Love Institute* founder and a practical spirituality teacher in Montreal, Canada. He is passionate about learning and teaching practical spirituality based on Rumi's teachings and those of other spiritual masters. He aims to promote peace and love in the world and to help people solve their life challenges using the power they possess within themselves. To learn more about the author and his books, visit:

https://www.PeaceAndLoveInstitute.com

Made in United States
Orlando, FL
04 November 2026

90204184R00139